CAPSTONE REFERENCE

BUSINESS
FAQs

BUSINESS FAQs

It is a fact of business life that most managers are promoted into their first management job with hardly any training. And if they get promoted again, guess what? The same thing happens again. Managers are basically expected to work out how to do a new job by reacting to the pressures the role puts on them. They can ask questions to begin with, of course, but by the time they have been in post for a while they find it difficult to reveal their ignorance or lack of skills to other people. *Business FAQs* comes to the rescue.

Business FAQs is:

- a one-stop shop, covering each individual aspect of your work.
- not too academic or theoretical.
- hard practical advice built on experience rather than management theory.
- a reference book that actually works.
- accessible and easy to use.
- simple and practical to implement now!

Business FAQs gives step-by-step solutions to sensible questions such as, *'What exactly is in a strategic plan?'* and *'How do you do risk assessment?'*

Ken Langdon and Andrew Bruce have taken advice and suggestions from a myriad of people, from their own colleagues to chef extraordinaire Delia Smith, to give us the answers to 100 of the most frequently asked business questions of all time.

From the difficult, to the sublime to the utterly ridiculous, *Business FAQs* will become your business bible – to be used in anger from day one and referred to throughout the rest of your career.

Capstone Reference provides the definitive resource books for the busy and information-hungry professional. Including Capstone's best-selling and completely revised *Ultimate* series, all Capstone Reference titles are up to date, relevant, robust, comprehensive and accessible.

CAPSTONE REFERENCE

BUSINESS
FAQs

ANSWERS TO THE 100
MOST DIFFICULT BUSINESS
QUESTIONS OF ALL TIME

KEN **LANGDON** • ANDY **BRUCE**

CAPSTONE

First Published 2002 by

Capstone Publishing Limited (a Wiley company)
8 Newtec Place
Magdalen Road
Oxford
OX4 1RE
United Kingdom
http://www.capstoneideas.com

CIP catalogue records for this book are available from the British Library and the US Library of Congress.

ISBN 1-84112-012-X

Typeset in 10.5/13 Minion by
Sparks Computer Solutions Ltd, Oxford, UK
http://www.sparks.co.uk

FSC
Mixed Sources
Product group from well-managed
forests and other controlled sources
Cert no. SGS-COC-2953
www.fsc.org
© 1996 Forest Stewardship Council

CONTENTS

ACKNOWLEDGEMENTS

A number of the processes and tools we use in this book are taken from the electronic tool set provided by Andy Bruce's company SofTools (www.softools.net). We would like to thank Mark Edwards, its technical director, for his extraordinary hard work and dedication.

Ann Trevor and Penny Ariff helped to input text; our thanks to both of them.

Our thanks to Richard and Mark at Capstone for their patience.

Our thanks also to Sheelagh Hughes at Editorial Solutions, as meticulous a copy-editor as you could hope for.

INTRODUCTION

It is a fact of business life that most managers are promoted into their first management job with hardly any training. And if they get promoted again, guess what? The same thing happens again. Managers and team leaders are basically expected to work out how to do a new job by reacting to the pressures the role puts on them. They can ask questions to begin with, of course, but by the time they have been in post for a while they find it difficult to reveal their ignorance or lack of skills to other people.

Perhaps you are in this position like so many others. Can a book help you? What sort of book would help? You need one that:

- is a one-stop shop, you don't have to buy a book covering each individual aspect of your work, you can have it in one
- is not too academic or clever, you don't need *Drucker on Globalisation* when you are trying to make a decision whether or not to hire someone in the Paris office
- gives hard practical advice built on experience rather than management theory
- is accessible and easy to use
- works.

We have set out to write just such a book. We have taken advice and suggestions from myriad people, not the least of which is Delia Smith who, amongst other culinary activities, writes cookbooks that really do answer questions in the way we talked about above. Ken came to an interest in cooking dishes beyond simple grills and stews late in life. So he looked at cookbooks. He wanted to do something more challenging than mince and two veg, so he looked for books that explained quite adventurous dishes, and hit a big snag. He kept running up against terms he did not understand. 'Now pour the mixture on to a griddle.' Easy if you knew what a griddle was, which Ken did not.

Other terms were familiar as words, but difficult to interpret specifically – 'parboil', 'sauté', and so on. Ken decided to abandon the cooking hobby and revived it only when he discovered Delia's *How to Cook, Book One*.[1] This contains recipes for quite advanced dishes, but also shows you how to boil an egg. So when you do not understand one of the terms used in an advanced recipe you can look for advice without changing books.

That is part of the model of this book. We are going to answer some tricky questions such as 'How do I get a buzzy, creative culture into my team?' but go back to the basics in the same book. I suppose the equivalent of Delia showing us how to fry an egg is our answer to the simple question: 'How do you assess the risk of a decision?'

Here is a simple risk assessment template as a sample answer:

Table I.1   Risk assessment template.

Ref	Risk	Probability	Impact	Action
A	What could go wrong?	How likely is the risk to occur?	How bad would the impact be?	What can you do to manage this risk?

The book also gives practical answers to **important** questions such as: 'How do I impress my boss's boss without annoying my boss?'

There is another part to the book model. Andy has been running his own company for a number of years. He has, therefore, been used to the fact that his role combined those of chairman and chief executive. Then Ken became the chairman of the company and we had to work out just exactly how that relationship would work – not only from a theoretical 'who does what' job description, but also in terms of the practicalities of decision-making. Decision-making is particularly difficult when only one of the two roles is present – for example when one of us is with a customer.

And this helped us to see life from the point of view of any team, be it the top of a large organization, a project manager or a first line manager. In each case there is a role defined as the chairman of the team and one called chief executive.

In the case of most teams the chief executive is the pusher and shover, the person with the vision and the entrepreneurial flair, concentrating on the short term and looking into their organization to see that people are making things happen. The chairman tends to be more detached and motivated to check out each idea, decision or process against a set of objective rules. The chairman looks outside the organization and thinks long-term. Then, of course, there is a third role. To succeed in business you have to work through other people – the human resources role.

The problem is the old one of balancing the pressures of today against the longer-term thinking required to build the business and it looks like this.

1   Without a long-term strategy companies run the risk that decisions they are making today will have a negative impact on results in the future.

2   But we have to stay real; business people are always under pressure to carry out urgent day-to-day tasks. They have to meet today's

objectives and overcome short-term problems. They have to respond to their customers, whoever they are. Everyone is involved in such work and in operational, or short-term, planning. In a fast moving environment it is little wonder that planning for the future tends to take second place.

3   You cannot implement any plan, short- or long-term without motivating people and building teamwork.

If these three statements are true for all organizations, they are more dramatically experienced in start-ups and small companies. There is no point in defending an action as being right for the long term if it is going to assist the business to run out of cash. On the other hand, making a sale that is outside the main route you have planned could be catastrophic for the future. And if people don't like working there, they will not stay.

So we come to the three heads, not necessarily chairman, chief executive and director of human resources – the three heads needed at the top of any team. A team needs a 'can do' and 'do it now' attitude. It needs someone who will discuss a problem, find a solution and immediately pick up the telephone to start implementing the solution. As for the solutions themselves, you should expect to need some fancy footwork just to keep things afloat. No one has solved the particular problems you are about to face; there is no precedent so one of the three heads has to spot solutions or activities that would be described by some managers, particularly in large companies, as completely off the wall. This role, the chief executive's, concentrates on performance.

And yet, and yet, no one built a business or a team without thought for the future affecting what we do now – the role of the second head – the chairman. In the end this role concentrates on process. It asks 'Do we have the processes in place that will make sure that the outside world does not change without our knowing about it? Do we have the health and safety processes in place that will keep us out of court?' and so on.

Finally there are all the complexities of issues involved with people.

Some people can simulate the three heads inside their one brain. Reacting, ducking and weaving with the best of them but also from time to time checking that they are not mortgaging the future or taking short-term measures that endanger the long-term goal. Others form teams of three where one person is clearly the go-getter, another the 'just a minute, let's think this through' and the third 'but can we take our people with us on this?'

So, here is *How to run your bit of the organization, Book One*, covering the hundred most frequently asked business questions of all time from the simple to the difficult, from the sublime to the utterly ridiculous – just like business life.

We need a working definition of the three roles. The performance-oriented person is probably the simplest to write down but certainly not the simplest to carry out. Form your objectives, plan how to achieve them and get on with it with no excuses.

The performance angle

Focus the team on what needs to be achieved, and get them to ignore anything else. Always ride your luck in all aspects of the job. If something has gone well, or a point you are making in a presentation has hit home, consider if you need to work in that area and drop some other activities you were going to do, or miss out other points you were going to make.

The process-oriented person should keep reminding themselves that they are chairman of the board, or the team, not the chairman of the company. Their role is to see that there is a well-oiled machine in place with all the bases covered. They have a role in understanding or even contributing towards the vision of the organization but they also have to ask questions about the process and procedures that are in place to operate effectively. Questions such as 'How are we going to make sure our decisions are the best ones available – and to explore the unknown and the future?', 'How are we making sure that we still understand what our customers really want? Are we asking if there any new types of competition around offering our customers another way of getting what we supply?'

The chief executive, performance, has to ensure the basics are in place, but the chairman, process, should challenge their fitness for the future. In some ways the conscience of the business, the chairman questions and challenges management thinking. You could call it continuous 'due diligence'.

The process angle

'*I am not afraid of a knave.*
I am not afraid of a rascal.
I am afraid of a strong man who is wrong, and whose wrong thinking can be impressed upon other persons by his force of character and force of speech.'
Woodrow Wilson, 1856–1924, 28th president of the US

Every part of an organization needs strong people, it also needs the disciplines and processes that make sure that Wilson's great fear can be avoided. It also needs the answer to the most frequently asked business questions, be they ones about flair and strength or ones about discipline and process.

We will try to answer some questions from the flair/leadership angle of the chief executive, some from the business process angle of the chairman and others from the human resources angle as well. And where it is a mixture of the three we will point that out too.

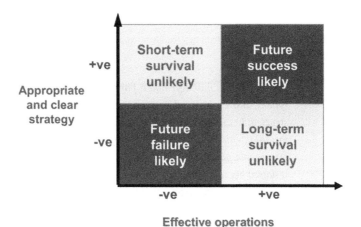

Fig. I.1 The long-term/short-term dilemma.

In the bottom left hand quarter the team lacks an appropriate long-term vision and is running inefficiently. It is likely to fail. Where we are all aiming to be is out of fire-fighting mode and in the top right hand quarter with good long-term vision and effective operations.

One of the problems with management is that one version of a right answer to a situation may be in conflict with another possible answer. You may be preparing to make a decision that is highly tied into your performance or your team's. But, there may be a people angle that would militate against a decision aimed solely at performance. Thirdly, the situation may have arisen because there is a process problem, in which case you have to decide whether to put in a quick fix, or take time to alter and bring up to date the business process involved.

The performance angle

Where it is useful we will illustrate the points that we are making with examples that are driven by performance.

A hassled sales manager was trying to implement a computerized sales forecasting system. It was a reasonably simple system, but he required the agreement of the IT department before he was allowed to load it on to his sales force's laptops. This was put in the queue of new programmes awaiting attention, and it looked as though it would not be up and running until after the man's next promotion. He sought advice from the supplier of the software, who suggested that his people access it on the supplier's web site. All that was needed to do this was the latest version of a popular browser. The salespeople already had this installed, and the sales manager was able to get the forecasting system working within two days.

The people angle

The same sales manager had a particular style of writing proposals. He put in a system that encouraged everyone to write proposals to a template that he constructed. In almost all cases it was successful, and his people reacted well to the new formula, which they found made proposal writing quicker as well as better. Except for one salesperson who dug her heels in and refused to use the template saying that it slowed her up and was not as good as the proposals she had been preparing previously. The sales manager noted that this salesperson was very successful and spoke to one of her customers about her proposals. Having had a clean bill of health from the customer, the sales manager agreed that she should continue with her own style. 'She is a good seller,' he explained to the human resources department, 'and geniuses make their own rules.'

The process angle

This sales manager had a lot of problems. He had taken on board two new people at an interval of three months. They both came with a hearty recommendation from the human resources people as the graduate trainees most likely to succeed in his particular sales environment. Neither of them fitted in to the team or succeeded. The sales manager decided that this was not a matter of chance, and asked to look at the process the human resources people were using to allocate trainees. He found that the skills and knowledge required in the job description had been valid some time ago, but that his business had changed. He was now involved in selling whole system solutions rather than commodities, and that was a different type of sell. He agreed with human resources how to change the vetting and allocation process and redirected the two trainees into more appropriate roles.

Notes

1   Delia Smith (1998) *How to Cook, Book One*, BBC Consumer Publishing (Books).

Section 1

CONCERNING THE BASICS

Introduction

The starting point for any person trying to become a better businessperson is to have the resolution to change things. If you are buffeted by chance and driven by external pressures you are surely in fire-fighting mode, a situation that is probably not viable in the long term. Next realize that the job of all managers and team leaders is to make decisions and exercise good judgement. We will look at the process of making decisions, and present a suggestion for documenting this process. Then we will consider those events in which businesspeople spend a lot of their time – meetings. Well-planned meetings can be a major aid to managing a team, not to mention managing your boss. The resolution to change, along with good decision-making and meeting techniques are like the stretching exercises of a fitness regime – they prepare you for moving on. Then you can focus on what you are trying to achieve and look at the outline of preparing a plan that enables you to get there. That's what this section is about.

Question 1 *What happens in the long run if I never get out of fire-fighting mode?*

There are two possibilities – either you will die first or your organization will. You will die first either literally, through stress, or booze if that is what you use to alleviate the stress, or you will die metaphorically because your boss will finally get someone in to do the job properly. Or your organization will die first either because it ceases to be a viable unit, or because your bosses reorganize things so that you are not such a danger.

The test of how deeply you are in fire-fighting mode is to compare the amount of time you spend on dealing with the cause of business problems with the amount of time you spend on the effects.

Example

Your washing machine is leaking. Finding the cause is not a complex process; you follow the water trail from where you saw it back to its source. It's a hose. It has frayed a bit and obviously leaks water, not all the time because when you got to it the machine was empty and the leak more or less dried up. You decide that the leak is very small and stick a bowl under the hose to catch the drips, vowing to check it from time to time and empty it if it is nearly full. Your decision is aimed at the effect. It has solved the problem with the least amount of effort and time. It could be that you will forget to empty the bowl and the floor will get wet again, and it could be that the leak, if unfixed, will get worse until eventually the hose bursts dramatically and you have a major flood. But that is for the long term. Put differently, the bowl under the leak is curing the effect, replacing the hose is tackling the cause.

This book will give you a lot of clues about how to get out of fire-fighting mode. Start by testing yourself to see how badly you've got the 'bowl under the leak' disease. How many decisions have you made in the last few days that are quick fixes as opposed to changes that will avoid problems or exploit opportunities in the future? Then think about your activities in another light. Are you working on issues that are important to your performance or mainly on issues that are seen as urgent?

In an ideal world your plan would be so good that you would only be working on issues that will have high impact on your team's performance, but are of low urgency at the moment – see the top left box in Fig. 1.1. Have a look at how much of the activity you are involved with today is in the top right hand box – high impact and high urgency. These are your crises. If

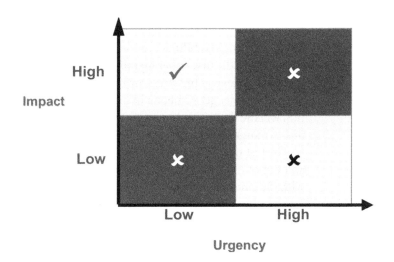

Fig. 1.1   The impact and urgency matrix.

most of your work is in the top left box you should avoid the crises of the future.

Question 2   ## Are decision-makers born not made?

The chief executive officer (CEO) bits of our minds have a tendency to answer this question positively. They argue that some decisions are split-second gut reactions to situations in which going through any decision-making process would result in wasted time and a decision, whether right or wrong, taken too late.

In fact, most decisions have more implications than it seems at first, if you take that attitude. Managers often make decisions without knowing they are making a decision at all.

Consider this domestic situation. Someone has stolen one of the two cars that Kevin and his partner Jean use. What actually is the decision they have to make? We eavesdrop on their conversation.

Example

Kevin: We have to decide which new car to buy. In fact I can narrow it down further. We have to decide which new sports car we are going to buy. I have always wanted a sports car and this is the opportunity to get one.

Jean: You have already made four decisions: that we are going to replace the car with another one, that it will be a new one, that we are going to buy it and that it will be a sports model.

Kevin: So?

Jean: So, the downside of what you are saying is that we will have to invest more, probably a lot more, in cars. The insurance claim will not cover a new sports car, we are still paying mine off and there are other things that we need. Surely before we go shooting off to buy a Ferrari we could take some other options into account?

Kevin: You just don't want me to have a sports car. Oh, and we are not going to spend the insurance money on a stair carpet.

Jean: Kevin, I am quite happy for us to have a sports car provided we have thought the issues through, including those of finance. Now what problem does not having a car cause you?

Kevin: I can't get to work.

Jean: Kevin you take the car to the station each morning to avoid the 25-minute walk that you used to take before we had two cars. If you went back to walking you would be getting the exercise that you say you are not getting at the moment and we would benefit financially from having only one car.

Kevin: There was another reason why I stopped walking. When it rained I was arriving at work soaked to the skin and with my trousers looking as though I had just crossed a muddy field, which in fact I had.

Jean: When it rains, I could take you to the station in my car.

Kevin: But what happens if it's raining and you have had to set off early for an appointment?

Jean: Then you take a taxi. It takes a lot of taxi fares to come to the same total as running a second car.

Kevin: Yes, but there are other times when we both need cars.

Jean: That's true, but there are not many. When it is unavoidable, it is almost certainly still cheaper on those occasions to take a taxi, or maybe, in extremis, borrow my brother's car.

Kevin: Wait a minute, if we go this way I will have to drive your little dinky car down to the rugby club. I couldn't stand the shame.

Jean: Think about it, Kevin. If we sell my car and add that to the insurance money we will have no further payments to make on that car so we could afford a better car like, well, a sports car.

Kevin: You mean we have to decide which sports car to buy.

Jean: Yes.

Kevin: But that's what I said in the first place!

Jean: Oh, darling, you are clever. (Flings arms round Kevin) And, with the money left over we could replace that filthy old stair carpet we inherited from the previous owners.

It may be that some people are naturally better decision-makers than others; certainly it is our experience that some people are confident enough to make a decision while others prefer to have them made for them. But whichever you are, you can level the playing field by using a decision-making process. Here is one that has an emphasis on a team making a decision. What it does is structure the conversation so that the best decision can be tested against others in a logical fashion.

The title of the decision reflects what you or the team has to decide. For example, 'We need a training course that …', 'We have to decide how to approach the small business market', and so on. Then you move on to identifying concerns.

In a formal decision-making tool you will need the first column as a unique identifier of the concern. Then you need to express what that concern is. Now go to the third column and work out what impact that concern is having on performance. Be as specific as you can at this stage and try to quantify the impact. The next two columns give a weighting to each concern in terms of Impact and Urgency. A simple numbering system of one for low impact and urgency to ten for very high impact and urgency gives a graphic statement of how important these issues are to the organization. You should try and limit the number of current issues to three. Any more and it will be hard for you to get your head round the implications of what you are doing and probably means that you have more than one decision to make. This discipline also means that you concentrate on the real issues, and get rid of

CRITICAL DECISION

Name	
Team	
Date	
Status	

TITLE

ISSUES

	CURRENT CONCERNS	IMPACT ON PERFORMANCE	I	U
I1				
I2				
I3				

OPTIONS

	OPTIONS	KEY FEATURES	S	A	F	E
A						
B						
C						
D						

EVALUATION

	SELECTION CRITERIA	P	A	B	C	D	PxA	PxB	PxC	PxD
1										
2										
3										
4										
5										
6										
7										
8										
9										
10										
						TOTALS	0	0	0	0

DECISION	

ACTION

	IMPLEMENTATION PHASES	OWNER	TARGET	ACTUAL	S
A1					
A2					
A3					
A4					

FAQ Tools.xls Page 1 of 1

Fig. 1.2 Critical Decision-making tool.

those with less impact on performance. Make sure you have a good understanding of the impact of the decision on the performance of the team, so that you focus decision-making on critical issues.

Once you understand the issues you can start to think about the various options available to deal with them and start the movement towards a creative decision. People often find it hard to find options. Their gut feeling tells them what needs to be done and they more or less pre-empt the decision-making process by defining one option in a way that makes it seem a more likely solution than any other. Most achievers think this is a mistake.

Despite the paucity of choice that Henry Ford famously made available to his customers – 'You can have any colour you want as long as it is black' – he trained his people in the opposite, and insisted that any decision that anyone was going to ask him to make had to have alternatives.

Most managers are faced frequently with 'there is no alternative' proposals. Indeed most managers find two things about people coming to them for a decision. First of all, they always ask for more resources. Secondly when they want a decision they generally have compelling and urgent reasons why the one option they are offering is the only one that meets the need, and suggest that any further exploratory work would stretch decision-making past the 'window of opportunity' after which it will be the end of life as we know it. This leads to this extraordinary limbo where everyone knows exactly what to do to solve crises, but no one has any ideas about how to avoid them.

The people angle

There is a phrase for this situation:
   'If I have to make a decision today, the decision is "No."'

Here are three good questions to help the creative options process.

- If there are no alternatives to this decision, how is it going to play a part in preventing similar problems arriving in the future?
- If I told you that this decision is unacceptable full stop and no arguments, what would you do?
- Have you asked three other people with experience in this area if they know of an alternative?

The SAFE boxes in the critical decision process stand for **S**uitable, **A**cceptable, **F**easible and **E**nduring. This is a good rough guide to how likely the option is to be implemented successfully. Is the option suitable for my organization given the current situation and strategy? Will the people whose support I need to implement the option be likely to find it acceptable? Is it feasible, can we actually make it happen given time and resource constraints? And finally, will it endure for a reasonable length of time, or are we likely to be back for another option in the near future? Use some measure against each of the options – perhaps red, amber or green to suggest the degree of suitability and so on. This gives the first rough cut of the decision, and then we need to move into the detailed evaluation of the options.

Once again we will number the selection criteria in the first column for ease of identification at this and later stages in the process. Then we come to the selection criteria themselves.

Try to use words like 'maximize' and 'optimize' in the statement of criteria, as that way you get a comparison between the options. The point here is to make criteria clearer by suggesting that you want the highest, or the biggest or the smallest. This technique takes practice.

It is also a good idea to add to the criteria the 'ideal' answer to each criterion. It may not be possible to meet these ideal statements, but at least it gives you something to aim at and again the ability to make comparisons. It is useful when using this document with stakeholders to show where your proposal is hitting or missing what the team believes is the best.

We now need a method of comparing the likely performance of each option against each criteria using the form.

The column marked P is for the team's estimate of the Priority of each criterion. Mark it from one to ten with one as a low priority. Remember to come back to this frequently as you identify and score more criteria. One you set at eight to begin with may later have to be adjusted down as two others are judged as being more important than it.

Remember that it is all relative. Look for a benchmark priority then adjust the others to it. Be prepared to revise the whole list if a new priority comes into focus.

Now use the next four columns to note, on a scale again of one to ten, which of the options A to D is nearest to the ideal. The next four columns simply multiply the criterion priority with its score to produce a number that reflects both the priority of the criterion and how nearly, comparatively, each option hits the ideal.

The totals at the bottom give the result of this evaluation.

Let's be clear. If you use the evaluation template particularly in a team environment, then you will have documented the logical thought that you and the team have put into making the decision. You have not necessarily made the decision. As you look at an option that is not at the top of the scorecard, you will see where it fails against an important ideal – one where the priority on the criteria is high and the performance of the option low. This gives you an opportunity to improve it. You may be able to change the result by making an alteration to the option.

Besides all that, do not forget your gut feeling. If the scored evaluation seems wrong, go over it again to make sure the logic is not flawed. If the score prefers an option that is a highly unexpected winner, you may find some misunderstanding is tipping the scorecard irrationally.

The performance angle

Lee Iacocca (b. 1924), former Chrysler chief said:

'If I had to sum up in one word what makes a good manager, I'd say decisiveness. You can use the fanciest computers to gather numbers, but in the end you have to set a timetable and act.'

This may seem a rather whimsical example, but it comes from real life, and is a reminder at this stage that in the real world managers do have to make quick and sometimes almost instantaneous decisions.

Example

You are the assistant manager of a small branch of a bank. It is just after lunchtime, and you are preparing yourself for the afternoon's meetings when your secretary comes in and reports that one of your biggest customers has just walked into the bank and is moving towards the only cashier on duty who, the secretary happens to know, is a bit drunk. You happen to know that the customer is a member of the local temperance lodge and is frequently seen on Sundays on a soapbox preaching the evils of drink.

How many options can you come up with in the time it takes for the customer to walk from the door of the bank to the cashier?

You could:

- *ask the secretary to go and tell the cashier that he has an urgent telephone call, and that you will take over dealing with the customer*
- *intercept the customer as he approaches the desk and usher him into an interview room to give him your 'personal attention'*
- *stand behind the cashier and be prepared to step in if something looks as though it might go wrong, although this may carry the risk that the cashier becomes abusive or even violent. Probably the phone call is better.*

How many more did you add, given the time frame? In the end you could always fall back on the old routine of sounding the fire alarm.

If you have used the SAFE model a number of times you will find yourself doing it intuitively, even in time-pressured situations like this.

Complete the decision-making process by recording the decision you or the team has made. Then move on to the implementation plan. Remember that a decision has not been made until implementation has started.

The people angle

An elderly painter and decorator was bemoaning his fate. He wanted to work less, and play a bit of golf, but the pressure from his customers to come and work for them was making this impossible. 'Have you decided to cut down the amount of time you are going to work per week?' said a process consultant. 'Yes, I decided ages ago but if I decide to play golf on, say, a Friday, I always have to cancel it because of work.'

'So,' came the advice, 'start the implementation of the decision by booking golf lessons in the middle of each Friday morning. At least that will cut your work down by half a day because you will not want to waste the money the pro charges you by cancelling at the last minute.' He did that and quite quickly stopped any work at all on a Friday. The decision did not really come into place until the action plan had started.

Question 3 *What is the difference between judgement and decision-making?*

What is the difference between judgement and decision-making? Perhaps judgement happens inside decision-making. When you are predicting the attitudes of stakeholders, or planning how to present your ideas to a doubter, you are exercising judgement. But good judgement is assisted in many ways by the application of the process we have discussed.

Perhaps judgement is decision-making without the facts, and you are going to have to do that sometimes. But the corollary is not true – don't ignore the need for facts. If the facts are available use a process to examine them rather than relying on a SWAG (a Strategic Wide-Angled Guess).

A Decca Recording Company executive in 1962 told a group that he was auditioning: 'Sorry we are not interested. Guitar groups are on the way out.' You will have guessed that the group he was turning down was the Beatles. He was reading the music fashion world wrongly and missing a quality ingredient of the group that the whole world came to recognize. I don't think any process would have kept the egg off his face.

Question 4 *How do I stop finding myself in meetings that seem interminable, are pretty boring and don't end up achieving much?*

Every successful person you speak to on the topic of management eventually stresses the importance of preparation. Every technique you look at, from managing people to managing projects, starts with doing the preparation work. About to go into a negotiation? Do your preparation. Need to fire someone? Prepare for the meeting and what comes after. And so it goes on.

The winner in every aspect of work is very frequently the one who did the most effective preparation.

Take a simple example – who are you more likely to hire, someone who at the interview knows what business you are in and who your competitors are or someone who guessed what you did and got it slightly wrong? We wouldn't think of going into an interview totally unprepared, would we? You take risks when you play things by ear, risks that you will look foolish, that the outcome will not be to your advantage and that someone properly prepared will stand out as more competent. Even time with a customer can be wasted through bad preparation.

Preparation is, therefore, the answer to the meetings question. Use a systematic approach to managing meetings that ensures that special or routine meetings have clear objectives, a focused agenda and appropriate logistics.

The objective is to ensure that time invested in meetings is efficient and worthwhile.

The principles behind this are that organizations and teams spend significant amounts of time in meetings (up to 50% of time available, depending on job type). Simple improvements in the way meetings are managed can have a dramatic impact on overall performance. Time and resources are consumed in meetings so it is necessary to ensure each one 'adds value' to all participants.

Clear meeting objectives will show everyone concerned the benefits to them of attending. Indeed if a person finds that the objectives of the meeting offer them nothing at all, then that is one boring meeting that they know to avoid. If you have difficulty getting this right, try starting with the phrase 'At the end of this meeting we will …' And then look for the actions that should come out of the meeting or the information that will have been passed on or whatever.

Now write down the people who are going to attend. For small meetings list the individual names, but for large meetings, reflect the different teams involved. Next formulate the agenda: the list of topics the meeting will need to cover to achieve the objectives. Some people like to put very detailed timings against each topic, while others are comfortable to let the discussion go on whilst concentrating on making progress towards achieving the objectives.

Before moving on from one topic to the next, make sure that someone has summarized and written down the actions decided upon, with who is responsible for carrying them out and when they are due to be completed. It is useful also summarize the points that were made in getting to the action plan; but often just the actions will do, and this keeps the record of the meeting as simple and concise as the meeting itself. Most people find that there is a distinct advantage in taking the minutes of the meetings they attend. It means you have to concentrate on what is being said, true, but it also means that any nuance of who is going to do what by when is up to you.

Finally ask yourself what logistics and resources are required in order to hold a successful meeting. It is a terrific waster of time if the first half hour is spent getting hold of the LCD projector, and the second half hour trying to make it work.

Just on this last point. Technology can improve the efficiency of meetings by, for example, enabling you to hold them remotely and keep the minutes on an internal or external network so that they are instantly available to everyone who needs to know.

The performance angle

'No fast track career was built on long meetings.'

Richard Humphreys, serial chairman

Question 5   *How do I get everyone to focus on performance rather than on excuses?*

You have two weapons in your armoury here. The first is to get financial targets in place that people have agreed to achieve over a specified period of time. This pre-empts the excuses, in that they agreed to have a go at these numbers in the first place. But these numbers tend to be the ones that the organization needs to meet its objectives and may have little to do with the environment in which a person is working. If, for example, a salesperson is measured by orders taken, they may very well succeed for a period of time, and then the results may fall off. They or their manager need to know that the downturn is coming so that they can do something about it. This leads a salesperson into another performance measure – the leads they are generating and the number of prospects they are working on.

Setting such indicators is probably easier for salespeople than for many others in the organization, but it has to be done. Each individual must identify their key indicators and set objectives for them as well as for the end results. The indicators have various names, including critical success factors – the factors that must be, and remain, in place for the team to achieve its objectives.

So, brainstorm the list of indicators and then prioritize them. This once again has the added feature of pre-empting excuses. You could try using a simple red, amber and green traffic light system to highlight priorities and urgencies. If there is an indicator a person feels is at risk, and it has a high priority, then something needs to be done now to correct the situation. You now have a new objective – to get that indicator under control.

Now, at regular review meetings you are in a position to look at the person's performance scorecard and continue to get your excuse retaliation in first. Don't forget to compare one team member's performance scorecard with another's to make sure they dovetail.

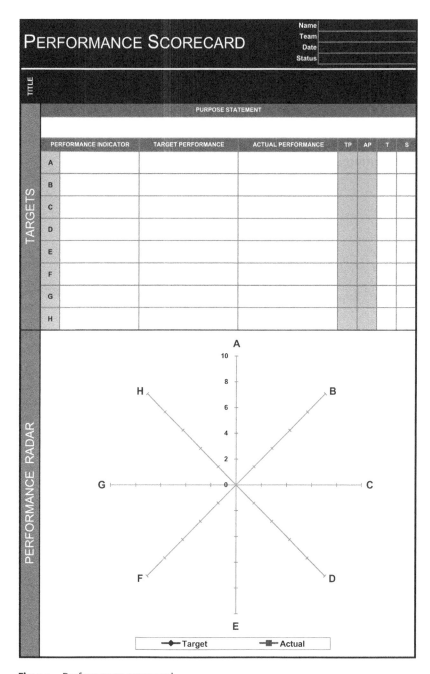

Fig. 1.3   Performance scorecard.

Question 6   **What, from a basics point of view, is the starting point of a business and its plan?**

This is a good question with some good subsidiaries, 'Do we really need a marketing plan?', 'What is a strategy?', 'What does customer-first mean?' and so on. We will deal with many of these topics in some detail in answering other questions, but thought it would be useful to give a short answer that sums up what you need to put the basics into place.

The actual basics are as follows:

- Know what/who your customer is.
- Know what products or services you are going to sell into which markets.
- Work out how you are going to handle each product/market making sure you know what differentiates it from its competitors.
- Put in place processes that implement the plan.
- Put in place a knowledge system that records where you have been, what you have done and where you might be going.
- Build the appropriate skills and capabilities into the team.

Know who your customer is

Whether they are internal or external you have customers. You had better know who they are because there is no other reason for you, your team or your organization to exist. Group them by whatever makes sense – small customers, individual customers or large organizations for example. This grouping simply distinguishes each type of customer so that you treat them differently and appropriately.

Know what products or services you are going to sell into which markets

Define these carefully into not more than about eight groups. Put in ones that are important now, and also ones that you are trying to get off the ground or that you expect your customers to want in the future.

Now build the products and markets on to an activity matrix (figure 1.4) giving you a series of cells that we will call product/markets. A product really has no value if it does not have a market, and similarly a market is a waste of time as far as you are concerned unless you have a product to take to it. So

Product/market	Product/ market 1	Product/ market 2	Product/ market 3	Product/ market 4	Product/ market 5
Market 1					
Market 2					
Market 3					
Market 4					
Market 5					

Fig. 1.4   The activity matrix.

think in terms of product/markets. You will quickly start to see that a similar approach to each product/market will not be entirely appropriate, so the next basic is to look at the way you will handle each product/market.

Work out how you are going to handle each product/market

Ask yourself why people will buy from you or indeed continue to do business with you. What will make your approach to each product/market successful? Think about how each customer within a market needs to view you and your products and services. Think how the competition is approaching each of your product/markets.

Put in place processes that implement the plan

This is where the chairman's role becomes key. Look at your strengths and weaknesses in approaching your product/markets and think about what you need to change. This gives you a series of change projects. Then look at all your business processes, summarize them as a chart of processes and start documenting and improving them.

Put in place a knowledge system that records where you have been, what you have done and where you might be going

You will have heard terms like 'learning organizations' and 'knowledge management'. There are two ways to start the process of using your experience and the experience of others to improve your performance. Either gather all the documents you can and make them as available as you can, or build a database of experience by using standard tools. This produces, over time, a huge body of knowledge that everyone can access and use. You are about to make a decision on what computers to put into your team – have a look at the standard template decision-making tools that other people, wherever they are, created when they were making a similar decision. Not only do you see what the final decision was, but also, more importantly, you see the logical process they went through to get to the decision.

Build the appropriate skills and capabilities into the team

Don't forget the people angle. Many a brilliantly conceived and carefully documented plan has come to grief because the team simply did not have the skills and capabilities to implement the plan. Both of us have been in the disappointing position of reviewing a team plan with the team's senior management, only to find after the team has left the room that the senior people did not think that the team was able to carry out the plan. The question has to arise, 'Why are you letting them try if they cannot succeed?'

So, these are the basics. You will get a lot more detail on how to do most of these tasks in other parts of the book.

The people angle

Human resources people are more aware than most of the individual's wish to be part of a team. Try making your team proud of the fact that they have the basics well in place by involving them in the planning activity and ensuring that good techniques, such as meeting preparation, are not optional but part of the team's unique quality.

Section 2

DEFINITION OF TERMS

Introduction

Most business books, and we have to include this one, generally suggest that managers keep their language as simple as possible and avoid jargon. This does not mean, however, that you will not have to have a working definition of the jargon that other unenlightened managers use. This is a fashion business. Words come into normal management speak and go out again. Indeed it is remarkable how some words proliferate amongst the entire business community for a period of time. A good example could be found at the strategic level when the gung-ho '80s gave way, through the early recession, to the more cautious '90s. During the '80s almost every company's strategy had words like diversify, expand by acquisition, add skills to head office. The '90s' key words became: return to core business, expand organically or by acquiring similar businesses, strip down head office and empower managers. The late '90s, early 2000s make us add words like globalization, continuous improvement and strategic innovation.

This section ignores, in the main, such fashionable phrases and concentrates on terms that managers need to understand because they have withstood the test of time. Some terms like Economic Value Added (EVA) are widely used but still regarded by some with cynicism, so for safety's sake we have included them.

Question 7 *How do you define value for money?*

We will come back to this when we look at the processes involved in selling, particularly business-to-business selling, or selling within an organization, but it is worth looking at this as a basic skill in dealing with customers. Here is a true story of an independent consultant that makes this point well.

Example

For many years Tom, not his real name, had offered consultancy services from a company that consists only of him. He is a one-man band. He did a planning job once for a big electricity company. The job was phase one of three phases and Tom and the customer completed it successfully. Indeed the main customer sponsor was delighted. When it came to phase two, the amount of money at stake meant that according to their purchasing rules they had to go out to tender. Tom's sponsor was pushed towards inviting in McKinseys who, at the time, were doing a lot of work at holding board level, as well as getting Tom to bid. Tom was working with two operating company boards.

Now, since they had used Tom's processes for phase one, it made almost no sense at all to change consultants for the second part of the project. Tom knew this, of course, and decided to go in at the highest price he dared. He really loaded his quote and waited for the reaction. It came in a telephone call from the sponsor. He sounded concerned and embarrassed and Tom feared the worst. 'Tom,' he said, 'I've got a problem with your price.' 'Oh my God,' thought Tom, 'I've overcooked it,' and he started stammering about how he could probably take another look at it. The customer agreed with this and suggested that he took another person on to the project to 'make it more of a team approach.' 'But that will make it more expensive,' said Tom. 'I know, Tom, the problem is you are more than £200,000 lower than the McKinsey quote. I can't take your number in as it is, the purchasing people will laugh you out of court.'

So, Tom took another guy on and shoved the price up to what was for him a stratospheric height. He got the business and, boy, did he holiday well that year.

What has happened here? Tom's original quote reflected the amount of time he had to put into the project and the price gave him a good return on that time. McKinsey went in at a price that reflected their knowledge, access to expertise and reputation. One could speculate at this time that neither bid really reflected the value that the project would bring to the customer. It is that value that eventually won the day.

So look at what you provide in terms of your customer's perception of value and you will understand how to approach them and how, if this is part of your function, to price it. The carrot for doing this, as we have seen, is that your value as perceived by them may be much more than you realize. The stick is that if you put a higher value on your performance than they do you are living in a fool's paradise and are risking losing that particular customer.

Question 8   *What is a discounted cashflow, and what is it for?*

Before coming to discounted cashflow, the main method used by most business people to calculate return on investment, take a quick look at the other methods used.

Payback period

This method measures the length of time from the first payment of cash until the total receipts of cash from the investment equals the total payment made on that investment. It does not in any way attempt to measure the profitability of the project and restricts all calculations to a receipts and payments basis.

Payback period

In considering alternative projects it is the one with the shortest payback period that is preferred.

	Project 1	Project 2
Asset cost	£10,000	£15,000
Net cashflow		
Year 1	£2000	£3000
Year 2	£3000	£4000
Year 3	£3000	£6000
Year 4	£4000	£8000
Year 5	£10,000	£2000
Payback period	3.5 years	3.25 years

In this case the second project would be preferred despite the fact that the positive cashflow for project 1 ramps up in the fifth year.

The payback method has the advantage of being quick and simple, but it has two major disadvantages as well.

1   It considers only cash received during the payback period and ignores anything received afterwards.
2   It does not take into account the dates on which the cash is actually received. So it is possible to have two projects both costing the same, with the same payback period, but with different cashflows.

The payback method giving poor advice

In this example the two projects have the same payback period. However, it is obvious that, without any further information, we should prefer project 2 since the cash is received earlier, and can therefore be reinvested in another project to earn more profits.

	Project 1	Project 2
Asset cost	£10,000	£10,000
Net cashflow		
Year 1	£1000	£3000
Year 2	£3000	£3000
Year 3	£3000	£3000
Year 4	£3000	£1000
Year 5	£4000	£4000
Payback period	4 years	4 years

It is in fact very difficult to know which of these projects is better for the business simply by using the payback method of investment appraisal.

The payback method has some disadvantages, but is still in use for quite complex projects. This is particularly true where there is a great deal of early capital investment in infrastructure followed by a lengthy period of income derived from those assets. A telephone operator is a good example of such a company, where the initial investment to lay down the network of cables takes time and costs a great deal of money.

Return on capital employed (ROCE)

It can be argued that an improved version of payback is arrived at if you average out the benefits stream over the life of the project. That is what the return on capital employed does.

Return on capital employed

Asset cost	£10,000
Estimated residual value	NIL
Expected earnings (before depreciation)	
Year 1	£2,000
Year 2	£3,000
Year 3	£5,000
Year 4	£7,000
Year 5	£8,000
Total	£25,000
Net earnings over 5 years	£15,000
Average earnings	£3,000
Average return on capital employed	30% (£3,000/£10,000)

It is sometimes argued that the average capital employed of £5000 should be used instead of £10,000. On this basis, the answer to this example would be 60%. Either method can be employed as long as this is done consistently.

Once again, however, return on capital employed has the disadvantage of not taking into account the time when the return is received. Thus it is possible to have two projects having the same ROCE but one project starts immediately, and the other has a pre-production period of say, two years.

Discounted cashflow

We are agreed then. We need a method of investment appraisal that takes into account the timing of the cashflows as well as their absolute amount. Discounted cashflow does just that. Look at it this way.

When would you like the money?

Suppose we offer to give you £1000. Would you prefer to have it now or in five years' time? Obviously now, since if you want to spend the money it will be worth more now than it will be after five years of even modest inflation. But what if you don't need to spend it now? Then you still want the use of it so that you could put it somewhere it will earn money. You will therefore have more to spend in five years' time.

But, you have assumed that we are paying no interest in the five years. Suppose we say that if you take it in five years' time we will pay you 50% per annum interest. Now, of course, you would prefer to wait. In five years' time we will give you £7593.75. Even if you needed to spend the money now, you could borrow it and still have a hefty profit in five years.

The concept of discounted cashflow is based on the usefulness of being able to calculate what interest percentage we would have to pay you for it to make no difference at all whether you take the money now or in five years. We know it is somewhere between 0 and 50%

The mechanics of discounted cashflow

To arrive at a method of doing this, consider the following.

You have inherited £10,000 from Aunt Mary. Unfortunately, she had heard that you are liable to spend money fairly freely so the will says that you cannot receive the cash until your 30th birthday. You are 27 today (happy birthday!).

Aunt Mary was actually fairly well informed. You are desperate to get this money before lunchtime tomorrow in order to place a bet on a horse someone has told you is going to do well in the 2.30 race. You have found a friendly banker who will advance you part of the money.

The interest rate is 10% per annum and she is prepared to advance you an amount, A, such that with interest you will owe the bank exactly £10,000 in three years' time. How much can you get?

If you borrow £100 now, you will owe interest of £10 by the end of one year so the total outstanding will be £110. During the second year, interest will be charged on the total amount outstanding of £110 i.e. interest of £11. The total outstanding would be £121. During the third year, interest will be charged on the total amount outstanding of £121 i.e. interest of £12.10. The total outstanding would then be £133.10.

We can see therefore that for every £100 borrowed, £133.10 must be repaid.

Therefore, solving the equation:

$$A \times 1.331 = £10,000$$

will tell us how much can be borrowed now, i.e. about £7510. This technique can of course be generalized to deal with any rate of interest and any time period.

We can now develop a method to compare two projects. Cashflows due in the future may be converted to equally desirable cashflows due today using the above method. This technique is known as discounting and the equivalent cashflow due today is known as a present value.

Table 2.1   Discounting.

Timing of cashflow	Amount of cashflow	Discount factor at 10%	Present value
Immediate	(£10,000)	1	(£10,000)
After 1 year	£3000	0.909	£2727
After 2 years	£4000	0.826	£3304
After 3 years	£5000	0.751	£3755
After 4 years	£3000	0.683	£2049
Net present value			£1835

Discount factors may be found from tables or by using the formula:

$$1/(1 + i)^n$$

where i = discount rate, and n = number of years.

In particular, consider the discount factor used above for year 3, i.e. 0.751. When deciding how much we could borrow from the bank in respect of Aunt Mary's bequest we divided £10,000 by 1.331. It is an exactly equivalent calculation to multiply £10,000 by 0.751 – the discount factor for 3 years at 10%.

The final result takes into account all cashflows by totalling them and is known as the net present value of the project.

If compelled to choose between two projects, we will select the one with the higher net present value. If we have a large number of projects all of which can be undertaken, then we would wish to invest in every project with a positive net present value.

Question 9   What is hedging?

'Here's a farmer that hanged himself on the expectation of plenty.'

Macbeth, Act 2 scene 3

You may remember the opening of the book by ex-Salomon trader Michael Lewis, called *Liar's Poker*. John Gutfreund, the Salomon chairman, comes out of his office and offers to bet $1 million on a single game of liar's poker with another senior manager. The bet goes 'One hand, one million dollars, no tears.'[1] The 'no tears' is to emphasize that the bet is for real and that the loser will not whinge about his loss. Indeed, get a group of city types together and they will find something to bet on. Wherever there is a degree of uncertainty, for example of supply and demand, someone will take positions on it.

The concept of hedging rears its head in the futures markets in which 'bets' are taken on the value of commodities or shares some time in the future. The history of what is now known as the derivatives markets goes back to some very sensible 'insurance policies' taken out by farmers. If you are dependent on crops that only grow once a year, you are dependent first of all on the vagaries of demand. How much cocoa will the chocolate manufacturers buy and use over the next one or two years? There is also risk to supply as it depends on what the weather is going to be like.

Cocoa is a traditional futures market, which started trading in 1926. Commodity suppliers sell some or part of their future crops forward. That is, they agree a price and a volume of product with a trader before all the uncertainties become known. In the cocoa market the timing of this is up to 21 months ahead. Farmers can now sleep soundly knowing that a proportion of their income is protected whatever the outcome at harvest time. The great idea is as simple as that.

But, of course, then the complications cut in. Producers have an interest in concealing the true size and condition of their crops. News of impending shortages will drive prices up; the prospect of a bumper harvest will take prices in the opposite direction. Since there is active trading in these futures, the original buyer can sell the contract on at a profit or loss.

Usually producers work out just how much of the crop they want to sell forward so that if there is a shortage and higher prices are available they will be able to take advantage of these for at least some of their produce. The proportion which is 'hedged' or 'insured' limits the risk to whatever level the producer deems acceptable.

The chocolate manufacturers are also playing a careful game. Their wish is to guarantee a minimum amount of cocoa whilst at the same time trying to achieve the minimum average price they can. They will buy forward only if they think the price is likely to rise.

This is the classic role of the commodities futures market, providing a way of hedging risk due to uncertainty about the supply and demand for basic materials and the pricing consequences which follow.

The great idea of hedging has been expanded to allow futures trading on stocks and shares. In this way an investor can buy call options at a price set at that time for a trade to occur at a fixed time in the future. Either side in this transaction can thus increase the potential reward of a share price rise by using gearing. It works like this.

Suppose you believe, for whatever reason, that the price of shares in GEC is going to rise over the next few months. You can buy an option in the futures market. Take these numbers as an example.

The share price of GEC is currently 658 pence. You believe that it could rise some 10% over the next three months to 725 pence and you have £2000 to invest. In this example I am going to ignore the costs of dealing to keep it simple. Remember every trade you make, whether in actual shares or options, is accompanied by a cost which will have the affect of reducing the numbers you are about to read.

If you buy shares in GEC and your prediction is correct you will make £200 or 10% in three months, which is not bad. But suppose you want more. You could buy a call option for 31p that gives you the right to buy shares at 650p in three months' time. Your £2000 buys you about 6450 calls. When the price goes up to 725p you can buy for 650p and sell for 725p at the same time. Your sale profit is 6450 × (725 – 650) or £4837, from which you subtract the original £2000 you paid for the option leaving a profit of £2837 – more than fourteen times the profit earned in trading in the underlying shares. You have received return on your original capital of an outstanding 140% in three months, a huge reward.

But a huge reward implies a huge risk. If the market goes against your prediction the outcome can be dire. In effect you are buying the shares for 650p, the option price, plus 31p, the price of the option, making a total of 681p. If the price is below that you lose. If the price in three months is 665p then your losses are 6450 x 0.16 or £1032 and you have lost half your money. If the price drops below 650p, of course, then you have lost the lot. The only people who cannot lose, of course, are the ones taking commissions on each transaction.

This principle of hedging and speculating can be applied to almost anything in the stock market. You can, for example, hedge or speculate on movements of the main market indices such as the FTSE 100. This means that your portfolio is protected if you were thinking of selling shares at a given point in the future. You can bet on spreads of prices and so it goes on. If you need an insurance policy, hedging is a great idea, but if you decide to speculate be sure you do it with money you can afford to lose. Most financial advisers steer their clients away from speculating in futures because of the huge risks, but as long as you can write the money off when you place the bet, it's an excellent return if you are lucky. But don't forget what the man said: 'No tears.'

As well as in the finance area, the concept of hedging has a place in a business plan where a manager decides on two courses of action with balancing risks. So, a production manager may phase new technology into half the production lines. That way they hedge the risk of the new technology being unreliable, with the certainty that they can continue production with more proven methods. They get half of the productivity benefits but without the risk of stopping altogether.

Question 10   What is responsibility accounting?

Companies have a major problem in devising an internal financial reporting system that really lets individual managers understand their performance to date and also allows senior managers to allocate the overheads of the business, of which they are a big part, fairly. If they get it wrong they can set up a situation where managers individually take decisions that are in their interests because it suits the management accounting system, but actually against the overall interests of the organization. The answer to this lies in responsibility accounting. You need to organize your management accounting system so that managers can truly control their profitability, make their contribution to overheads over which they have control, but not burden them with overheads out of their reach. It might look like Table 2.2 (opposite).

But it can still go badly wrong. Head office must allow that their costs, which are apportioned to the divisions, must make some sort of contribution or be cut. Here is what happens if the head office believes that its costs are inevitable and fixed.

Example of responsibility accounting going horribly wrong

In this case head office costs of £24 million are allocated to divisions by turnover.

Division	A	B	C	Total
Turnover	100	50	50	200
Divisional contribution	18	7	5	30
HO costs	12	6	6	24
Profit	6	1	(1)	6

The long-term viability of division C is plainly not there and the decision is taken regretfully to close the division. By definition head office costs are unaffected in total and need to be re-allocated.

Table 2.2   Responsibility accounting.

	Divisional management accounts	Note	Product A	Product B	Product C	Total
	Sales	1				
minus	Variable costs	2				
=	Contribution	3				
minus	Fixed costs controlled by division	4				
=	Contribution controllable by manager of division	5				
minus	Fixed costs incurred by division but controlled by head office	6				
=	Divisional contribution to head office costs	7				
minus	Apportionment of head office costs	8				
	Divisional profit	9				

Note 1: These are the division's sales recorded by product.

Note 2: These are the variable costs of producing the products sold.

Note 3: We call sales minus variable costs the contribution. This gives a measure of the relative profitability of each product.

Note 4: The fixed costs over which the divisional manager has complete control.

Note 5: Controllable contribution. This is a fair measure of the success of the divisional manger and we can use it for evaluation purposes. The division's managers will use it to get a proper estimate of implementing new ideas or reacting to an unexpected opportunity. Such decisions are not affected by similar decisions being made in other divisions.

Note 6: An example of this might be the information technology costs incurred if head office gives the division no right to go elsewhere for this service. The same could go for transport or facilities. Similarly if head office controls the decision over investment in fixed assets for the division, then the depreciation figure will appear here.

Note 7: This contribution is a good indicator of the short-term viability or success of the division. We can look at making more costs controllable by the division or remain convinced that head office should remain in charge of these costs. At least we can see them.

Note 8: There are some costs that are not incurred by the division but have to be paid for. In here we would find the costs of the board itself and possibly the human resources department. The term apportionment indicates a recharge on a fair but arbitrary basis – possibly based on sales turnover.

Note 9: This bottom line gives us a fair measure of the long-term viability or potential of the division.

Division	A	B	Total
Turnover	100	50	150
Divisional contribution	18	7	25
HO costs	16	8	24
Profit	2	(1)	1

Oh dear, now division B faces the chop.

Division	A	Total
Turnover	100	100
Divisional contribution	18	18
HO costs	24	24
Profit	(6)	(6)

Neat, eh? By refusing to believe that head office costs were not directly linked to the contribution of the divisions, we are forced, once again with great regret, logically to close the business. A silly example but you can see the point.

Question 11   What is operating leverage?

One more point on the use of management accounts. There is a huge benefit to be gained if a division or a company can increase its sales volumes without increasing its fixed costs. It illustrates what managers are often talking about. 'We have to sweat the assets.' When you have spent money on infrastructure of any sort, slight increases in sales have an unexpectedly high impact on the bottom line.

The concept of operating leverage shows the benefit of this.

The performance angle

Operating leverage

Look at the impact on the bottom line of different splits between variable and fixed costs. Each of the four profit and loss accounts is built to answer the same question. 'If we can increase sales volume by 10% without increasing fixed costs what % impact will it have on net profit?' Operating leverage is calculated by dividing this percentage by 10%.

First case

	£	£
	Current	*Additional 10%*
Sales	*100*	*110*
Variable costs	*90*	*99*
Contribution	*10*	*11*
Fixed costs	*0*	*0*
Net profit	*10*	*11 (an increase of 10%)*

The operating leverage is 1, i.e. there is no leverage at all.

Second case

	£	£
	Current	*Additional 10%*
Sales	*100*	*110*
Variable costs	*60*	*66*
Contribution	*40*	*44*
Fixed costs	*30*	*30*
Net profit	*10*	*14 (an increase of 40%)*

The operating leverage is 4.

Third case

	£	£
	Current	*Additional 10%*
Sales	100	110
Variable costs	30	33
Contribution	70	77
Fixed costs	60	60
Net profit	10	17 (an increase of 70%)

The operating leverage is 7.

Fourth case

	£	£
	Current	*Additional 10%*
Sales	100	110
Variable costs	0	0
Contribution	100	110
Fixed costs	90	90
Net profit	10	20 (an increase of 100%)

The operating leverage is 10.

As always the upside potential of leverage is matched by the downside risk. If you have operating leverage of 5, then a 10% improvement in your sales will produce a 50% improvement in your profits. A 10% drop in sales will produce 5 times that decrease in profits.

The impact of leverage has another dimension when you look at it in terms of dependency on customers. It is quite possible to lose an important customer. Suppose your biggest customer does 20% of your business, but because of operating leverage. Losing that sales turnover would wipe out your entire profit. It can easily be the case.

Question 12   What are the main financial ratios that help to understand the financial health of a company?

An essential driver of business is its performance against the most common ratios used by boards of directors and shareholders. Here are eight ratios that are frequently used.

Return on capital employed (ROCE)

This is often considered to be the main indicator of the profitability of a business. After all, the basis of enterprise is to take money in the form of share capital and loan capital and use it to earn profits. This ROCE percentage is a good guide to the performance of managers in producing sufficient return. A sudden alteration for better or worse will give rise to further investigation to see what has changed.

Profit margin

This shows the profits made on each pound of sales. As businesses grow, their managers are concerned over time to maintain a good bottom line profit margin. It is quite reasonable that peaks and troughs will occur. For example, where a company has been involved in a major expansion, it may take some time, measured in years, to get back to its original profit margin and then exceed it.

Return on assets

This ratio is more important in some industries than others. Basically the clue is the amount of investment in fixed assets required to create a going concern. In a firm of consultants, for example, where there are few fixed assets since arguably the main assets are the people acting as consultants, this ratio will have little relevance. In the case of a telephone company with the hugely expensive asset of the network, this ratio is crucial.

Return on shareholders' funds

This ratio measures management's ability to use the share capital in the business efficiently and produce good returns. There is a tendency to use this measure as a final measure of profitability. In some ways it is a more logical measure of return than ROCE, since the latter ratio is lowered by the inclusion of loan capital in capital employed. Some would argue that because the interest on loan capital has already been deducted from net profit before tax, then the providers of the loan capital have already had their return and should be excluded from the capital employed. That is the case with this ratio.

Economic value added (EVA)

This is also known as economic profit, and is defined as the difference between net profit after tax and the cost of the capital employed in the business. This is said to be an important indicator of managers' real created value. It certainly has a benefit internally as managers who are targeted on EVA are forced to realize constantly that all capital has a **cost**.

Market value added (MVA)

Very much linked to EVA, market value added takes the market capitalization of a business and subtracts the total of its capital employed. Assuming this is positive, MVA is said to put a value on the 'stock market wealth created'.

In summary, EVA tries to show the return to shareholders on an annual basis, while MVA attempts to show the total return.

Added value

This is the difference between the market value of a company's outputs and the cost of its inputs. An improving trend here should augur a successful performance. The main problem is to get the necessary data to make the calculation from published material.

Total shareholder return

This measures the return to shareholders from dividend income and capital gains in the value of the shares. It can take time into account by discounting income and gains made to present value, and is a very useful tool of comparison between one share and another.

Question 13   ## What is e-learning?

The term stands for electronic learning and refers to self-development using training programmes made available over the internet or over the corporate intranet.

Learners first identify their personal development needs, and then work through online material as and when convenient to them. On completion, they are able to take a simple test to validate that they have learnt the basic concepts and can apply them in the work environment.

The most effective form of e-learning is when it is combined with face-to-face training in what is called a 'blended' solution. E-learning offers the advantages of being able to reflect the different learning styles of individuals, as well as offering the potential to reduce the overall time and cost of training.

Question 14   ## What is knowledge management?

Quite simply this means getting the right information to the right people in the right format at the right time. The term 'knowledge' differentiates between data of no relevance and value to the business, and information that addresses a clear business need – knowledge.

The process of managing knowledge often involves technology to make information available through a central store or database where others can easily and quickly access it. For this reason the IT community often own knowledge management – although increasingly companies are placing operational managers in charge of this essential area of the business.

The benefits of effective knowledge management include improved sharing of learning across teams, and reduced rework caused by repeated mistakes.

Notes

1   Michael Lewis (1989) *Liar's Poker*, Hodder & Stoughton General.

Section 3

DEALING WITH CUSTOMERS

Introduction

Right, so far we have agreed that the starting point of any plan is thinking about how to approach your product/markets. This involves communicating with customers be they internal or external. Start from the downside of all of this. If the top line of your profit and loss account, whether management accounts or the real thing, goes wrong, you are eventually going to have a problem. Lack of sales leads to good cashflow ironically since you are not spending on cost of sales but are collecting revenue for precious deliveries and this sometimes fools people as to how things in reality are. And lack of sales starts from lack of prospects and lack of a successful selling effort.

So there is a bit of every businessperson that is in fact a salesperson. Whatever you are, a project manager or, dare we say it, a member of the finance department, there is part of your function dependent on being a salesperson with good communications skills. We will deal with this in two sections. This one is about the starting point of being a salesperson working on the defining core of their role – persuading people to act in a way that allows the salesperson to achieve their objectives and keep their performance scorecard clean of status red performance indicators.

Selling is, of course, a good example of the need for the performance or chief executive approach and the chairman or process-driven style. We recently heard a senior figure in the health service saying that a disciplined salesperson is a rarity. Not in our experience. Successful salespeople are generally professional, good planners and well disciplined, though they sometimes hide this by adopting the sales swagger that they did it all by force of their personalities and a series of hot dinners for the clients.

Question 15   *What is the most important basic skill in selling?*

Lots of people get this wrong. They talk of the gift of the gab, a smooth talker who could sell sand to the Arabs and refrigerators to the Eskimos. Selling sand in a desert or refrigerators to a person living within the Artic circle is simply not possible, however smoothly you talk, besides which no self-respecting salesperson would accept such an incredibly difficult sales patch.

No, every successful person we have talked to has given the art of *listening* a prominent role in successful and persuasive communication.

Active listening is indeed a great art. Unfortunately the voice most people like listening to beyond all others is their own. Fortunately, however, this is a useful aid to the salesperson who can take advantage of this and do the opposite – spend a considerable part of their business life listening. If you are trying to get someone to agree to something they will actually tell you how to do it if you ask them to talk about their requirements and desires. In the end you are trying to link what you want to what they want – so listen, for goodness sake and find out what that is.

Don't leap in with your views in meetings, particularly customer meetings. Listen until everyone has spoken, assimilate what has been said and eventually summarize the substance. By that time you will know where your interests lie and be able to steer the meeting towards them.

To illustrate this, here is an example of someone determined not to communicate but finding it in the end impossible to stay silent.

The people angle

A manager overheard one of his salespeople talking to another just before he carried out her annual appraisal. 'I am not going to say a word,' she said. 'This will be the shortest appraisal of all time.' Fat chance. The manager asked two open questions that enabled her to talk about that most interesting of topics – herself – and she was off.

In his book *The Seven Habits of Highly Effective People*, Steven Covey puts the point beautifully.

The process angle

'Habit 5: Seek First to Understand, Then to Be Understood.

The habit of communication is the most important skill in life and is the key to building win-win relationships. We typically seek first to be understood. Most people do not listen with the intent to understand; they listen with the intent to reply. They're either speaking or preparing to speak. They're filtering everything through their own paradigms. In contrast, Emphatic Listening gets inside another person's frame of reference. You see the world the way he or she sees it, you understand how he or she feels. This does not mean that you agree necessarily, simply that you understand his or her point of view.'[1]

Open questions are the ones that cannot be answered in one word. They generally start with how, why, what, who, where or when. Prepare to ask a few and settle back to listen.

Listen actively. Someone described a good listener, whom we both knew, like this, 'He seems to give you his undivided attention.' Encourage people to talk with your body language and the occasional interjection. Listen also for what is behind what is being said. If a customer says 'I do not think it is necessary to take action on this,' they could mean that they cannot do what is necessary or that they do not know what action to take. You will hear the difference if you polish up your listening skills.

Question 16	*How do you balance time spent delivering products and services with finding new prospects to sell to?*

If your customers place orders and require delivery you will get busy, so busy that you can end up buried in the delivery or customer satisfaction part of your job, and ignoring the task of finding new clients – a vital part of your future. Indeed when you go into a new job you will find yourself fire-fighting and working long hours just to survive. That is when you forget about the order book.

It's particularly difficult if your background is in production, marketing or finance and the emphasis you put on working does not naturally push you towards broadening your customer penetration. One of the advantages of coming with a sales background is a complete understanding of the disciplines of prospecting.

Salespeople also know that when you are selling you are not delivering and earning revenue, and when you are delivering and earning revenue you are not selling. It is easy to let your business life reflect this in a cycle – easy, but dangerous. A hole in the order book now is a hole in the cashflow in about two months' time. This delay can give you a false sense of security especially when you are busy delivering and finding it hard to fit in what needs to be done in that part of the business, let alone adding selling time. But that is what you must do.

Set aside an hour each week for prospecting – finding new clients – or more if your business demands it. During this hour make your phone calls or send out your mail shots or devise your new brilliant gimmicks for generating potential customers. Never, ever miss it out. Some salespeople always do it on a Monday morning since that tends to be the time that other salespeople are in their weekly meetings or touching base with their offices or whatever.

Don't waste prospecting effort. If you send out a mail shot and you are in a business where you need to follow up with a phone call, most businesses don't send a huge number out at the same time. Send out enough so that you have sufficient numbers to ring to fulfil your prospecting quota. This drip feed technique has the added advantage that you have to go back to it on a regular basis, thus automatically putting the hour a week discipline in place.

Question 17   *Who in the team needs to talk to the customers?*

Easy one this – everyone. The way to keep your team in touch with reality is to allow very few of them to be completely unexposed to customers. You can do this individually by insisting your product developer, for example, attends customer progress meetings, or en masse by inviting the customer to come and speak at the annual get-together. Engineers, for example, sometimes completely transform the way they think about their work when they come to have a real insight into what the customers are trying to do, and how they look at their offerings.

Suppose you run the financial control department for a function based in several locations none of which is in your building. You would not consider trying to do that without going to see the staff on their site to get a feel for what they are contending with. But if you do not get some of the accounts people out there as well you are failing to tap into an important source of insights. If the accounts people get out there as well from time to time, they may well see activity going on at the site that could be assisted by a simple change in how they carry out their tasks or a modification to their processes that you have missed because of your lack of intimate knowledge of the details.

Question 18   *What is the best way of handling price objections?*

Despite looking at your value from the customer's point of view, you will probably be in a competitive situation in which case the absolute price is a contentious issue.

'Sorry, mate, I've found a cheaper quote.' What do you do when you hear these words? The best advice sounds rather contrary – welcome price objections. After all if they are objecting to the price it sounds as though they think the product or service might do the job. And you will be more likely to manage the situation well if you appear confident. Breaking out in a cold sweat will harden the objection rather than loosen it.

And price is getting more and more important in everybody's business. Intermediaries and consumers, using the Internet, can trawl for the cheapest price. The question 'How do I stop the sales force giving away discounts?' gives an example from the insurance industry where a broker has hit a price objection.

Consider the possible replies to the customer's statement about your price. 'We'll match it' gives big profit problems. A reiteration of the features and benefits of the salesperson's proposal sounds heavy, is probably boring, and clients are unlikely to be swayed at this stage. In any case, at this stage they think that an alternative offer is similar. Much better is to drive back to the customer's basis of decision. Try the return question 'If we were the same price as the quote you are preferring just now, would you buy from us?'

What is the client to say? Suppose they say, 'Well, no actually,' the worst outcome, at least you can now ask why, and deal with the other objections real or imagined. Suppose they say 'Well, yes, I think we would.' At that point the question 'Why?' will elicit what the client believes are your advantages as opposed to your general statements. In this case clients are almost persuading themselves that the bit extra is worth it. Incidentally, the other selling technique that is tested by this method of handling price objections is the ability to remain silent and listen. Frequently the 'Would you buy from us if we were the same price as the cheapest?' question leads to a lot of thought from the prospect. Keep your mouth shut and wait for the response.

Incidentally, if you have done a good job at question 15, that is, listened well, you will know the answer to the 'Why' question better than the customer. It is still a better technique to let them state it than to table it yourself.

Question 19   *Is there a template for writing a customer proposal?*

If you have spent a lot of time and effort getting to the stage where a customer wants a proposal, it is a great pity if the document you submit or the presentation you make does not take the sale forward to the desired conclusion. In fact, in the opinion of many people, good proposals and final presentations do not often make the sale on their own, but they have often stopped the sale stone dead.

This answer to this question is yes. It's what a lot of people think is the most important template of them all – the communications template. This template works if you are sending a letter or an e-mail, making a presentation or simply talking through an argument aimed at getting someone's agreement to a course of action. The easiest way to explain it is to take a specific example and the one we have chosen is the executive summary to a sales proposal. But to repeat, the same formula works if you are trying to persuade a secretary to let you talk to her boss, a bouncer to let you into a full club or a member of the opposite sex to do whatever it is you have in mind. (Or the same sex if that is what you prefer.)

The communications template as an executive summary

The executive summary is a selling document. It gives the customer's general management teams a summary of what the supplier's proposal is. We use it to inform and persuade high-level customer managers, and we should be happy for the chairman or chief executive to read these documents. We should also be sure that they would understand from them what we are proposing and what it means to them, the customer.

Length

According to basic professional sales technique, the summary should be between two and four pages, and generally more towards two than four. Many senior executives ignore proposals of over two pages, knowing that someone else will read them in any case.

Style

The most important attribute is that it should have a readable and interesting style. After all, we are hoping that senior managers will spend the three or four minutes it takes to read the document, and end up knowing what we are proposing, what it means to them and how long it will all take. They will also know what the financial implications, both costs and return, are likely to be. This is vital information for such an executive, and it is a tragedy if our writing style makes them put the summary down without finishing it.

Timing of writing

At the time you are planning the overall sales strategy, it should be possible and beneficial for you to write down many elements of the summary. It may of course change considerably as the campaign progresses, but it is a good check that you have thought through what you are about to do.

Executive summary data sheet

This template is as relevant to an internal selling document or report as it is to an external one.

Begin to prepare the data sheet the moment you have identified a sales campaign and agreed to carry it out. The sooner in the campaign you can answer the questions it raises, the clearer will be your strategy. This gives you selling focus and allows you to brief all the managers, product experts and commercial people involved in the campaign so that they act consistently and support your overall approach.

It is unlikely for any campaign that you will have a full and satisfactory answer to every question, but the nearer you can get to that, the more likely you are to win the campaign, and equally importantly, the easier it will be to produce an interesting and compelling executive summary for your senior customer managers.

This is an internal document but contains everything you need to produce the executive summary for delivery to senior customer managers towards the end of the campaign.

Background

This makes them trust you as a salesperson or account manager, in terms of your having done the appropriate work and spoken to the appropriate people. You must mention some of their people that they trust. They are also immediately aware of what you are recommending. Perhaps more than

THE W.I.S.E TOOL		Name	
		Team	
		Date	
		Status	

TITLE

BACKGROUND

SCOPE OF PROPOSAL	WINNING STRATEGY	VALUES	
		One-off costs	
		Annual costs	
		One-off benefits	
		Annual benefits	

	CUSTOMER NAMES	ACTIVITY	AGREEMENT	S
C1				
C2				
C3				

OPPORTUNITY/PROBLEM

	OPPORTUNITY OR PROBLEM STATEMENT	I	U
O1			
O2			
O3			
O4			

BASIS OF DECISION

		SELECTION CRITERIA	CUSTOMER 'IDEAL'	S
FINANCIAL	1			
	2			
	3			
PRODUCT/SERVICE	1			
	2			
	3			
PRACTICAL	1			
	2			
	3			

Fig. 3.1   Executive summary data sheet. (*Continued.*)

PROPOSAL	PROPOSAL ELEMENTS		ONE-OFF	ANNUAL
	Product			
	Service			
	After sales support			
		TOTAL COSTS		

BENEFITS		BUSINESS BENEFIT		ONE-OFF	ANNUAL
	TANGIBLE	Increased revenues			
		Reduced costs			
		Avoided costs			
			TOTAL BENEFITS		
	INTANGIBLE	Management control			
		Customer satisfaction			
		Competitive edge			

IMPLEMENTATION PLAN		TASKS	START	END	Q1	Q2	Q3	Q4	Q5	Q6	Q7	Q8
	T1											
	T2											
	T3											
	T4											
	T5											
	T6											
	T7											
	T8											
	T9											
	T10											

NEXT STEPS		RECOMMENDED ACTIONS	OWNER	DATE
	A1			
	A2			
	A3			

Fig. 3.1   *(Continued.)*

anything it demonstrates that your organization understands a lot about the customer's business.

Scope

This explains the boundaries of your proposal. As succinctly as possible it states what the opportunity or problem is that your customer is facing. It also shows how this proposal addresses the problem or opportunity and suggests the main benefit areas.

Winning strategy

This is a short statement of why your organization will win this particular piece of business. After discussion with your team you should be able to identify the unique thing that differentiates your proposition. Once you have got this it is a useful tool for communicating the strategy to anyone involved in the campaign. Do not be surprised if this strategy changes during the campaign.

Costs and benefits

You will, of course, be able to enter the capital and revenue costs of your proposal as two single figures. The challenge is to be able to total the benefits that you have agreed with the customer. This depends how close you have got to the people making the customer's business case. They are probably not the same people who will do any product evaluation. Your knowledge of the business case is a good demonstration of a supplier behaving like a collaborative partner rather than a supplier of commodities. Many large organizations have stated that they wish to create this type of relationship with their strategic suppliers.

Customer name, activity and agreement

Here you state the names of the customer's people you have worked with in preparing the proposal. In the actual summary document it will appear something like: 'We would like to thank Tony Phipps for his work in attending demonstrations and agreeing the technical viability of our proposal. Anna Heward gave us a lot of assistance in preparing the outline of the business case, and Ian Goddard gave us vital inputs to the implementation plan. Our thanks to all of them.'

Under the headings on the data sheet put down the key people you worked with, what you did with them and what they have agreed that helps your case forward. The status box should be marked red, amber or green to show how far you have got during the campaign to get these important agreements.

The customer problem or opportunity

After reading this managers will understand in more detail what the proposal is for, and will have a snapshot of the business benefit that will occur.

When we are selling to a customer, we are either solving a problem or allowing them to exploit an opportunity. State that here, with a reference to a person or a document to support the impact and urgency of the need.

Problem or opportunity statement
Explain in their terms what problem you are solving with this proposal or what the opportunity is that you are helping them to exploit.

Impact
In the summary you will comment on what you have been told of the impact of the problem or the significance of the opportunity. If necessary, you will mention the names of the people who gave you this information.

Urgency
This records how urgent it is to solve the problem or how significant it is from a competitive point of view for your customer to exploit the opportunity.

Value
For each statement give an indication of the value of the opportunity or perhaps the cost of the problem.

The basis of decision
Now that they know the problem or opportunity, we need to show them that we can see the decision to go ahead from the customer's point of view. In effect we are telling them what to look for in our submission.

This section shows that you understand the issues affecting a customer decision to go ahead. It is normally useful to divide it into three sub-sections:

- financial – a statement of the customer's criteria for investment if appropriate
- product – a statement in customer terms of any product or technical considerations
- practical – a statement of the practical implementation issues that shows that you are aware of them.

Selection criteria
This is a statement of each decision criteria. Try, during the sales campaign, to discuss these with the appropriate people.

Feature of the 'ideal'
Put down here what you have found to be the customer's ideal under each criterion. We may not be able to match it exactly, but this ideal will shape how we write the criterion in the executive summary itself. It is also useful

when using this document internally to show where our proposal is hitting or missing exactly what the customer wants. The winning strategy must feature here, perhaps in different words – you are seeing it from their point of view. Prove that the customer needs what is unique about the supplier's proposal.

Status
Again red, amber or green to show how much work we need to do to get nearer to the ideal.

The supplier proposal
This is a simple statement in customer terms of what we are proposing they buy and do. It tries to avoid jargon. After they have read this they will know what you are proposing.

Proposal elements
Keep it simple and high-level. This is not the section that describes each feature and part number of your solution. Think of it from a senior manager's point of view. What does he or she need to know?

Capital
The capital costs of each element.

Revenue
The revenue or ongoing costs, probably on an annual basis.

Benefits
This gives them a clear of idea of the business benefits and who, in their organization, is taking responsibility for achieving them.

Business benefit
A statement of the customer business benefit. To get to this it is often useful to keep asking the 'so what?' question. Write down the benefit. If it is difficult to see the connection between the benefit and a monetary reward to your customer, whether or not we can quantify that, ask: 'So what?' Eventually you will get to a simple statement of the real benefit. Try to use the sub-headings to avoid mixing up solid financial benefits such as a reduction in an existing cost from less tangible, and therefore less compelling, benefits such as an improvement in management control. Add in your unique benefit under whichever heading it fits.

Implementation plan
You and the customer, either separately or together, will probably have a project plan by the time it comes to writing the executive summary. Boil it down into at most ten actions or groups of actions. Remember the purpose

of this section is to give senior management confidence that the people concerned have thought the project through well enough to ensure that there is a high chance that the implementation will be successful. In the actual document you will convert this into a Gantt chart.

Recommended actions

The objective of the executive summary is to encourage and persuade someone to do something. This section records what those short-term actions are. In most cases your recommendation will include that the customer should place an order for some or all of the elements mentioned.

To complete this answer to question 19 could we suggest that you try it out? Think of an idea you want to get across to somebody at work or at play, and mull through the template. If what you are trying to persuade them of is simple then you might find that you hardly need more than 100 words to fill in the summary; if it is more complex you might find it becomes two pages or the equivalent in conversation. Try it with kids. If you keep it interesting enough to make them listen you will certainly overcome their logical resistance to going to bed. If they remain obdurate despite your organized diplomacy take their favourite gun off them and replace the recommended action plan part of the template with the parental stopper, 'Because I said so.'

Question 20   *How do you get a committee to make a decision?*

Many decisions in business are taken by a group of people, a committee or a board for example, and many a sale has been lost because the seller is unaware of the cup of coffee close.

The manager has made his pitch, or the salesperson his final presentation to a group of decision-making managers. It is the easiest thing in the world for the chairman to thank the speaker for making the case so well, and say that the managers will give it serious thought and discussion. The meeting ends with no decision because the chairman actually does want to hear everyone's views before a decision is confirmed. If they decide against, they can tell the salesperson by phone or by letter, always easier than face to face.

Pre-empt the situation with the cup of coffee close. If it feels good and the vibrations are positive, offer to leave the group on its own for ten minutes. 'Look it must be difficult for you to make a decision while I am here, I'll go and have a cup of coffee while you have a chat. I'll pop back in a few minutes.' Either they are going to agree to your suggestion, a buying sign, tell you it is not necessary for you to go, another buying sign, or they are going to say that it is not necessary for you to return and that they will get back to you in due course, probably a warning signal.

It's quite fun if they agree to your returning in a few minutes. If, when you return, everyone looks at you, you have got the order. If only the chairman is looking at you and some people are having their own quiet discussion you can be sure you have more work to do or that you have lost.

The performance angle

Here is the longest recorded cup of coffee close. A salesman had presented a complex solution to a complex production problem to the board of a medium-sized company. He felt he was going to succeed and used the cup of coffee close. After an hour, it being the end of a long business day, the managing director came out of the room and suggested the salesperson came back the following day.

He returned at 8.30 in the morning and found the group much as he had left it. 'Bloody hell,' he said. 'Have you been here all night?' They had been and he got the order.

Question 21   *What are the most useful closing techniques?*

It's as easy as ABC – Always Be Closing. We do not know who first coined this phrase but it's spot on. Ginger up your communication skills by practising and using good closing and trial closing technique.

Salesman: 'Which of the colours fits best with your kitchen decoration – the grey or the light blue?' This is called an alternative close.

Manager: 'If you had those resources would you take responsibility for achieving that objective?' Trial close.

Mother: 'If you had your own clothing allowance would you keep your room tidy?' Associated project close.

Teenager: 'But everyone's getting them, so if you don't buy me them now there will be none left.' Impending event close.

Notes

1   Stephen R. Covey (1990) *The Seven Habits of Highly Effective People*, Econo-Clad Books Library Binding.

Section 4

MAKING A PLAN, AND GETTING A TEAM TO IMPLEMENT IT

Introduction

Very few people work entirely on their own. Most people have to motivate and organize a team to meet their objectives. The performance and people side of this can be complex. Let's, however, look at the process side first and work back. An effective team needs a strategy that all its members buy into, but it also needs one that fits in with the organization's overall strategy. To get this right you have to start from understanding the top driver of your organization and then produce a team strategy that aims precisely in the same direction. So right at the top we will look at a key performance indicator for all quoted companies – the market value of companies, and then work down. Then we can have a look at some of the performance and people issues peculiar to team work.

Question 22   *How do investors value companies?*

Let's start by looking at the key driver that sets the strategy of a company from the top. A public company rewards its shareholders in two ways – the current dividend, and the expectation of future dividend growth reflected in the market value of the shares. Before you set out on the rocky road to a strategic plan, therefore, make sure that you are thoroughly familiar with how shareholders value companies. This may seem unnecessary at lower levels in the organization, but your bit of the organization is, in the end, part of the whole.

Don't let anyone tell you otherwise – the value of a company is based on the dividend stream it pays to shareholders now and in the future. At any given moment a company could be paying no dividends at all and still have a high value. But that value still stems from the fact that the company, or a successor company will pay out annual dividends to its shareholders sometime in the future. In the same way a team is judged by the value they add to the company's ability to improve its profit/dividend strategy, now and in the future. They do this by adding value to the product or service they offer to customers.

Now we go back to the main driver at the top. To pay a higher dividend you need higher profits and, of course, you need the cash to make the payment. Your strategy must in some way pay attention to those two requirements. If it does not make money and generate cash at some point in the implementation, it is not aimed at the heart of the company's purpose.

Investors are aware of the profits that the company made last year. That existing position is given by the yield, which is a comparison of the dividend paid last year with the value of a share. The yield reflects the current return. They then take a view on the management and their likelihood of being successful in implementing their plans for the future. This expectation of future dividends is encapsulated in the other interesting ratio from an investor's point of view called the **price earnings ratio** or the multiple. It simply records the market value of a share as a multiple of the company's earnings per share. If last year's earnings were £1 million in total and there are 1 million shares issued then the earnings per share is £1. If the investors who are studying the likely future performance of the company are paying £20 for a share, then the price earnings ratio is 20. The price earnings ratio gives us the market's view of the future prospects of the company.

Everyone uses the historic earnings as the basis for the price earnings ratio because that is the only solid number that everybody has. If investors have taken an optimistic view of the likely growth prospects of the company the price earnings ratio will be much higher than if they regard the prospects for growth as slow.

Look at the price earnings ratio of your organization, and as you approach your strategic plan be aware that the profits you plan and forecast must bear good comparison with the overall price earnings ratio. If you are in the core business of your organization and, for example, the price earnings ratio is 12, then make sure that the overall budget you plan at the end of the planning process shows a return on investment of at least 12%. This will reappear as the answer to another frequently asked question: 'What is a discounted cashflow and what is it for?'

Question 23   *What exactly do you mean by a strategy?*

The process angle

'The end product of strategic decisions is deceptively simple; a combination of products and markets is selected for the firm. This combination is arrived at by addition of new products markets, divestment from some old ones, and expansion of the present position.'

Igor Ansoff (b. 1918), strategy guru

The word strategy is possibly the most ill-used piece of management speak in the business. You will frequently hear middle managers complaining that their board of directors does not have a strategy. This is normally not the case. Their strategy may be wrong, their strategy may need to change to react to events, but they do have a strategy. Maybe middle management have not been told about it or maybe middle management have misunderstood it. It is, in fact, the definition of the board that they plan strategy. Indeed most people have a reputation as a strategic thinker before they get to the top.

Come down a few levels to team leaders in whatever department and the accusation 'they do not have a strategy' starts to look truer. It is difficult for team leaders to have an up to date strategy, particularly in organizations that do not give concrete guidelines on what a strategy is and how, and most importantly when, to review it. Difficulties abound.

- It is difficult for a team leader to build a strategy because it takes time.
- It is difficult to have enough information about the future.
- It is difficult because short-term pressures stop the team getting on with the job of creating a strategy and even if the team does, it frequently ignores the strategy whenever a customer or other significant pressure blows it off course.
- Your best strategy may be impossible because other parts of the business will not change to suit you.
- Building a team strategy needs consensus, which means that some team members are going to have to compromise over what they see as the best way ahead.

The process angle

> 'Look, everything is going to change, so what is the point in wading through a whole load of forms and documents in a customer development plan.'
>
> *Disgruntled account manager*

So, if it's difficult it must be an area where the return for getting it right is very high. Put simply, you need to build a strategy with your team, agree it with all your main stakeholders or interested parties including your customers and flaunt it. Anyone with an interest in, or a part to play in, or who has an impact on, your strategy is known as a stakeholder. We must mention communication again here because it goes through every phase of strategy building. Know who your key stakeholders are and give them good, continuous and well-targeted information at the right time.

The first skill involved is the ability to balance short-term thinking with long-term planning. Put it in your schedule. Make regular time to review your long-term prospects. You do not have much time; you needed a strategy yesterday. And, who knows, you may need a new one tomorrow. The time span between reviews depends on the business you are in and on external events such as competitive activity. The steel industry can afford to put in place a strategy and leave it more or less undisturbed for many years. The software industry may need to carry out major reviews of strategy twice a year. If one of your customers is taken over, or two of your competitors merge, you may need to review your strategy and announce it all within one day.

Here is some step-by-step advice for agreeing a team strategy. Start from what a strategy is not.

- The annual budgeting round. Don't mistake this for strategy. We will come to the budgeting activities when the rest of the strategy is well worked out.
- A large book of management speak containing mission statements of 400 words that attempt to cover all the aspirations of the management team without pausing for breath. Here is one of these at board level.

'Our strategic intent is to strive for leadership in the most attractive global communications segments through speed in anticipating and fulfilling evolving customer needs, quality in products and processes, as well as openness with people and to new ideas and solutions. Based on our resources including technological know-how, market position and continuous building of competencies, we are well positioned to achieve our future goals.'

'Yes, but what are you going to do?' you long to scream.

A mission statement like that recalls the old limerick:

> There was a young man from Milan,
> Whose limericks never would scan,
> When his friends asked him why,
> He said with a sigh,
> 'It's because I always try to put as many words into the last line as
>   I possibly can.'

Back to what a strategy is not.

- A document produced by a staff function, carried around only by the same people, who use it solely to demonstrate that what the line departments are doing is against the strategy.
- A matrix of numbers produced once a year and left on the shelf until such time as it is due for review.

Right, keep it simple, what is it? A strategy is a plan of what you are going to sell to what markets and how you are going to do that. The strategic plan allows everyone to know how they should do their jobs, what the boundaries are and how the team leader will appraise any suggestions for doing new things. It is the team leader's job to bring focus to the team's work and make sure that the results are actionable rather than business school babble.

Start from the selling idea. Whether or not your customer is internal or external to your organization, you have a customer. What is a customer? It's someone who buys your products and services. A group of customers is called a market, so a strategy looks at segments called product/markets. Think in product/markets rather than products and markets and you are on the way to having a strategy.

Here is a nine-step way for your team to build and agree a strategy in a reasonably short time – say two days' teamwork over four weeks, with everyone doing about two person days of preparation work in the same time period.

Strategic analysis

1　First work out where you are now and what is going to happen in your world in the future. Make a list of every trend or fact that will have an impact on what you are going to do. Trends are the most important part of this. Which way are products and services developing? What are the market's requirements over the next two years? You may have to take into consideration economic, legal and political trends. You will certainly have to think about technological changes and their potential impact on your plan. Now get the team to find out the facts behind every trend on the list.

Example

The chairman of a south-east brewery when presented with some ideas for the use of e-commerce in 1999 said, 'All this Internet publicity is a flash in the pan. It's just kids' stuff. E-commerce will never catch on in business.' Mmm.

2　Analyse your customers and your competitors. Write down the buying criteria that your customers use to decide whether to buy from you or the competition. This gives you what they think is important. Now write against each of the criteria what the customer would ideally like. If, for example, ease of use is an important criterion, then the ideal the customer might use is 'requires no special off the job training'. Neither you nor your competitors may be able to achieve the customer's ideal, but if you know what it is you have an aiming point. As objectively as you can, measure yourself and your competitors against this customer ideal. This will give you a series of threats, where your competitor is ahead, and opportunities, where you can see you have an advantage.

3   Now examine your internal capabilities. Look at your business processes, your information systems and your facilities and equipment. Finally look at the team and assess its skills and experience. This step will give you a list of areas where you need to make improvements.

4   Summarize the analysis using the SWOT analysis technique. Simply group all the key issues into the headings: strengths, weaknesses, opportunities and threats. Take some time to check your SWOT analysis with other stakeholders like your boss and your customers. You are now ready to make a plan.

Making the plan

5   Define your overall purpose. Why does your team exist? Keep it simple and clear. You are not here to 'exploit our knowledge of the food industry', you are here to 'sell bulk food and specialist foods to the European market (predominantly the UK) in the next two years'. Even this simple statement may take time to agree. Someone is bound to object, saying that if that is the purpose what is going to happen to the home delivery service and so on. But once agreed you have the first brick in the wall of strategy.

6   Now look for your competitive advantage. Once again this is a brief statement of why customers have bought and will buy from you rather than anyone else. If your customer is an internal one, then do not forget that they too have choice. Make sure that your competitive advantage of being in the same company holds water. There are a lot of out-sourced computer departments wishing their strategy had included thinking about that. If you honestly cannot think of your competitive advantage ask your customer. You should in any case check it over with the customer in a sensitive way.

7   Set boundaries. A strategy is not only about what you are going to do, it is also about what you are not going to do. Write it down and get everyone to agree to it. Tricky if it means ruling out some pet projects, or if you put one customer requirement outside the boundary when the salesman who deals with that customer is pushing hard for its inclusion.

8   Here comes the crunch. Choose the areas of emphasis in terms of product/markets. Once you know this emphasis you will be able to allocate resources accordingly. Take your activity matrix with your product groups down the left hand side, and your market groups across the top. Into each cell in the matrix put what the current emphasis is, whether high, medium or low, and what your future emphasis will be. You may get some surprises here, like finding that a

major area of resource is actually working in a product market that is fast declining. All good stuff, and your strategy is taking shape.

9   From this emphasis document, or activity matrix, you should be able to produce an overview of targets and budget: what value of sales you should strive for, what costs you will incur and therefore what profit you should expect. Incidentally, this overview should make the filling in of the annual budgeting forms very straightforward.

Throughout the process be prepared to question and challenge accepted norms. Successful team leaders fight tooth and nail before acknowledging that something the company is doing wrong cannot be changed. But watch the politics. It is a tough call, but you have to make a judgement on whether entrenched views held by your bosses can be challenged by you at this time. Many people find the safety-first 'agreeing with the boss' plan much easier to contemplate; so most people err on that side rather than taking the risk of becoming known as a doubter, or worse a troublemaker. *Courage, mon brave*, nobody said life was easy.

The process angle

The powerful people behind Marks & Spencer over its declining years in the nineties are a good case in point. Two of their strategies, the sourcing strategy and the marketing strategy, failed to keep up with events. Whilst companies like Adidas were combating the threat of bankruptcy by recognising the inevitability of using overseas suppliers, M&S doggedly pushed on with their 'Buy British' strategy. Similarly they clung to their 'No advertising' strategy until their market share had declined disastrously and the bad PR avalanche had more than halved the share price and, would you believe it, made them vulnerable to takeover. Eventual realization was too late and the top directors lost their jobs.

You have a strategy and, to prove it, it is written down. Tell people about it, partly because you are trying to build your career and partly because you want to influence others towards your way of thinking. Make presentations. Sell your methodology to others so that you become the source of the company-wide strategic planning system.

Include in your communications the performance scorecard you have created to measure success in implementing the plan (see question 5).

Finally exploit the fact that you now know the reality behind building a strategy; so when someone complains that the board does not have a strategy, confidently ask him or her to explain, 'What exactly do you mean by a strategy?' You will be amazed how many cannot say, or give you a line from a limerick.

Question 24   *How do we ensure that we implement our plans?*

A military man once observed, 'No strategic plan ever survived contact with the enemy,' and so it is in business. No strategic plan ever survived unscathed in the market place. Prepare to implement and change your strategy – this is the tough bit. You need a reputation as a strategic thinker, and you do that by building a strategy. But real credibility in this area comes from making it happen. The key is KISS – Keep it Simple, Stupid.

Define change projects

You will have discovered in setting the strategy that there are many gaps and problems in the way you do things now. A good SWOT analysis will point at the areas for improvement. They may be legion, so you will have to prioritize them. Once again a major benefit of implementing a strategy is that you decide what you are not going to improve as well as where you are going to take action. Boil the prioritized list down to a manageable size of five or six issues. Call each of these a change project and you should manage them just like that – as projects. Set objectives for the change and a timescale for it to occur. Put someone in charge of it and use your leadership skills to keep momentum behind the change projects even when day-to-day events threaten to swamp any longer-term thinking.

Learn from experience

Implementing change projects is an area bogged down in management speak. It is also an area where your humility needs to shine through. Ask for help. Somewhere in your organization someone has done something like it before. Learn from them. You may well do things differently with the information you have about your specific problem, but make sure you have learned the lessons from the past before setting off on a change project with little chance of success.

The people angle

In one large company a lot of change was necessary in order to move its culture from a state-owned monopoly to a competitive business. Management produced a screed of initiatives aimed at changing how everyone went about doing their jobs. The trouble was that there were so many that they were never properly followed through. A lot of work would be done in a staff function but what actually happened in the field was rarely touched. The wags on the shop floor gave the tidal wave of initiatives an acronym 'BOHICA'. This stood for 'Bend over, here it comes again'.

Write your bible

So, you have a series of change projects with objectives and timescales. Now draw up the strategy bible. This is a folder containing one page, if possible, describing each change project. On it will be the milestones you will use to check that the project is on track, the actions in a sensible level of detail, the owner of each action and milestone and the time by which it needs to be complete. Keep it simple so that monitoring the plan is straightforward.

Check the plan for risk

You are nearly ready to implement the strategy. But check it first for risks. You do not want to give publicity to a strategy that is eventually written off as BOHICA. Look for the downside. What could go wrong? What will you do if it does go wrong? Is there any contingency plan you can put in place to mitigate the risks, and so on? If any of your colleagues are genuine friends, or if any of your friends are competent, ask them to add their views to this part of the planning process. If you can defend it against them you have a copper-bottomed winner. We will say more about risk later on.

Review your operational targets

Now think about the linkage between a new strategy and operations. The new strategy should put you in a position where your results will improve. The changes you are making will result in higher sales or profit and improved customer satisfaction. This is your best lever for obtaining the other implication of the new plan – more resources. It is a well known fact of business life that if any person asks to speak to their boss it is because they want more resources in some way. Your new strategy gives you the opportunity to do this in a much more logical way than perhaps your colleagues are using. The logic you use is as follows: I will give you these improved operational results if you give me this increase in resources. Take care. Managers, particularly we find sales managers, are brilliant at agreeing to one side of your proposition but not the other. 'I like the results, we'll have them but you can't have the resources.' Make the linkage logical and absolute or they will at best water down the resources on offer and at worst just up your operational targets.

Review roles and responsibilities

The one certainty of reviewing and changing your strategy is that people's jobs will change. Agree these changes with them and alter the reward scheme if possible. Many a bright shiny new strategy has faltered on the simple proposition that the incentive scheme supports the old one.

If people need training, invest the company's money in it. Do not forget that when you are investing money in your peoples' training you are also investing it in your team's success. Offering training allows you to reward success, build personal loyalty and demonstrate that your part of the business is well enough under control that you can release staff for self-development.

Communicate the strategy

OK, it's time to go public. Whether or not you actually manage the strategy right through its implementation or not, make sure you get the kudos for its creation by telling everyone about it. Well, not everyone, but anyone who needs to know and is in some major or minor way impacted by the changes you are making. It is a rule of life that if someone's job is affected by a change in strategy they can stop it dead. But don't send everyone the whole plan. The warehouseman in Newbury does not need to see the whole illustrated document if the only thing it means to him is that his hours have changed from starting at 8.30 to stating at 8.00. Do an executive summary, take out appropriate extracts for different individuals and use presentations, if you are any good at them, but sparingly. You should by now have the agreement of all the key people to your plan; so tell people what is going to happen in order to make it more likely that it will happen.

Monitor the implementation

The way you have documented the plan should make this aspect relatively easy. Use a green, amber and red system in your and your people's reports. Against each operational target or each milestone in a change project ask the people responsible to report on at least a monthly basis. Your meeting agenda then consists of taking the red issues first and the amber ones second. Assuming that most of the plan is at green, review meetings will be focused and of reasonable length.

Then change it all again

The reality of strategic thinking and planning is that it never stops. Harold Macmillan when asked what his biggest problems were said, 'Events, dear boy. Events.' How very true. Keep checking the strategy to see if it is still relevant and feasible. Competitors come up with new ideas; technology changes and people leave one job for another. All of these and myriad more events require you to make changes to even the greatest strategy of all time.

Remember you need a reputation as a strategic thinker to succeed in a top job, but don't stay around too long – this events business is a bastard.

Question 25   *How do you check that your plan is feasible?*

You are not Superman. Take a cold hard look at the new strategy and implementation plan, and ask yourself: 'Can we do this?' If you have followed a logical process you will have produced the best plan. It means change and new challenges. Suppose it were to include the need for you to go scuba diving. Would you just get hold of the equipment and jump straight in? No, you would make sure you went to a reputable trainer and learnt how to swim underwater safely.

So it is with implementing strategy. Do you have the skills to carry it through? It probably needs an amount of project management. It may test your knowledge of financial techniques or take you into new areas of people management. You almost certainly do not have all the knowledge you need at hand or in your head. Are your computer skills up to it, or are you going to waste time by not exploiting technology to its optimum. Can you deal with senior managers who may get involved, by demonstrating that your strategy fits in with theirs?

Admit it if you cannot do something. It is much better to say you cannot do it. This makes you learn, adds to your skills and takes out some of the risk of non-performance. Everyone we have spoken to in researching this book emphasizes making sure that you learn all the time.

Question 26   *If the people are not up to implementing the plan do you change the plan or the people?*

Depending on the circumstances either of these courses may be appropriate. The action that is completely inappropriate is to keep both the plan and the people, and yet that is what often happens.

If you find it difficult to admit that you cannot do something your people will as well. Encourage them to talk about those parts of the strategy where they are less confident that they know what to do or know they cannot do. Then you can help them, or rearrange the plan to take that task away from them. We have both often been in conference rooms where a good strategy has been thrashed out, but it has been obvious that the current team does not have the skills to implement it. We have pointed this out and the team has made some modifications or made plans for self-development. Ken has even sat with senior managers brought in for the final presentation of the plan, and when the team has left the room they have turned to him and said, 'Great plan, Ken, but that lot can't do it.' It begs the question: 'Why are you letting them try?'

Question 27   *How do you get people to accept change?*

Good question, because generally speaking people hate and are frightened of change. For this reason managing change can be a depressing business but there is hope. There has been research in production and other environments to support a rule of thumb that we have found to be true practically. If you have to manage a change process you need 'agents of change' to support you. Agents of change are people who fundamentally agree with the need for change and have the will to go through the process themselves. The rule of thumb is that you actually only need 20% of the people involved in the change to be agents of change from the start if you are going to make it happen.

The people angle

A European electricity supply company was preparing to become a private company having belonged to the state all its life and was preparing strategic plans for all its power stations.

Senior management knew that there would be fierce resistance to the changes that had to be made, and they decided to include the whole management team of each power station in planning the new strategy. This produced rather large teams of up to twenty people, but seemed the right way to go. The resistance differed from station to station and a pattern emerged. In the more progressive stations where, say, 50% of the team could be regarded as agents of change either before the planning session or after it, senior managers could already see the first signs of successful change. If at the planning session the figure was 20%, it was harder work but it could be made to happen. Below that it looked and turned out to be hopeless. And of course there was one where no agent of change appeared, not even the station manager, and they failed there. So the rule of 20% is a practical one.

So, before you start out to implement change make sure you can name the agents of change and that their number obeys this 20% rule. Caucus with them if you have to, and explain their role in helping you. If you break up into work groups or task forces either in the planning or implementation phase, seed them in amongst the laggards. Incidentally, if you do not take charge of the groupings, the agents of change will work together and you will lose their contribution to converting the non-believers. So when you hear a depressed colleague talking about the daunting task of getting a hundred managers to change the way they work, ask him or her how many will be supportive to begin with. If there is more than 20% tell them about the rule and encourage them to go for it. If it is less than that number just leave him or her, politely, to get on with it. Don't get involved or you will find that depression is contagious.

Question 28   *How do you get people to feel they are part of a team?*

In his autobiography *Writing Home*, the playwright Alan Bennett gives an insight into different attitudes amongst team members. He differentiates musicians from actors. In the first case:

'Striking about the musicians is their total absence of self-importance.'

He describes how the musicians play a piece and then discuss amongst themselves as to how it might be improved. They make suggestions to each other directly, not via the director. Anyone is invited to comment, their views noted and in some cases adopted when they go to repeat the piece. According to Bennett this would be impossible with actors.

> 'No actor would tolerate a fellow performer who ventured to comment on what he or she is doing – comment of that sort coming solely from the director, and even then it has to be carefully packaged and seasoned with plenty of love and appreciation,' states Bennett.[1]

This is just what it is in business. In most teams the egos of the individuals get in the way of sharing suggestions. There are exceptions and they tend to be successful people. Watch out for them. They encourage openness and constructive criticism of everyone, by everyone. They tend to be very laid back, good listeners and very understanding of peoples' problems. When they are team members they are terrific allies of the team leader and still liked by their colleagues in the team. When they are team leaders they bring the best out of people continuously. They don't manage everyone in the same way, though, some of the team they can encourage to be musicians, and some will always be actors.

We look at aspects of leadership, an important ingredient in the answer to this question, elsewhere.

Question 29 *How do you build a team from scratch?*

This section of the book is about the processes behind organising a team; so it is appropriate to look at the different stages in the life of a team, like a project team brought together for a specific purpose for a specific amount of time.

A good rule of thumb is that teams go through six recognizable stages in their development. If you can recognize these stages and understand them, you will put emphasis on different team-oriented actions at the right time. Here is a summary of the stages, issues and some suggestions for what the team leader needs to do at each stage.

Stage of development: forming

Issues at this stage:

At the forming stage the team leader is making decisions on recruitment. They have to decide skills, the number of people, and what their roles in the team will be. Once they have a plan for this they get their resources through gaining budget and a commitment from their sponsor for the project to go ahead.

The key action here is to select the right people and get their unqualified commitment to see the project through. For more on this see the section on managing people, section 6.

When the team comes together there are fairly complex interactions between the people who are tentative and unsure about exactly what their role is compared to everyone else's. If some of the people have worked together before they will have preconceptions about each other and may well form a team within a team.

Remember they are concerned with what their own roles are and equally concerned about why others are there. It is a difficult stage and needs to be thought through carefully if there is to be a smooth transition into the project proper and the next stage of development.

Stage of development: storming

Issues at this stage:

A short time into the project people will recognize where their best interests may lie and start to jockey for additions to their responsibilities. They will be very interested, for example, in who is going to talk about the progress of the project to other stakeholders. Frankly this tends not to be constructive and at this stage the whole looks much less than the sum of the parts. With the best will in the world, people come to a new project with fixed ideas and prejudices. They will try to prove that their prejudices are correct and that they know best. Watch out in particular for how the team is listening to each other. In a difficult storming phase you will see surprisingly little listening going on at all.

The people angle

Suggestions to help with team building:

Demonstrate how teamwork is crucial to success. Form sub-groups of individuals who do not normally work together and ask them to perform certain tasks or write a short report on some issue. This is the time when lots of team leaders use team building courses and outward-bound events.

The keys here are communications and authority. Have a good explanation of the roles and responsibilities of each person and present it at an early team meeting. Where there are grey areas describe these and ask for suggestions from team members as to where responsibilities that might fit into more than one role should go. Then use your authority to agree on the most appropriate. Defuse conflict at this time and show that you are going to use openness as your weapon for dealing with political manoeuvring.

Stage of development: norming

Issues at this stage:

This is the time when working practices and processes are agreed and put in place. The team agrees how they are going to work together and what the team ground rules are. Teams will naturally adopt 'norms' but it is important that the norms they adopt reflect best practice. For this reason the team leader has to be proactive in driving best practice into project processes.

Agree on how the team will communicate and how key decisions will be made. Start the process of team decision-making by demonstrating, perhaps at a regular team meeting, the decision-making process in action (see question 2: Are decision-makers born not made?). These norms, plus the team's approach to risk assessment and risk taking, become the team's operating principles.

Push this through to a good logical conclusion with no loose ends. Foster team spirit and agree on the development of the skills of each member of the team. At this stage it is important that each person sees that as long as the team is successful they are going to come out of it better people with increased competencies and capabilities.

Stage of development: performing

Issues at this stage:

The team is now working positively towards agreed objectives, milestones and performance indicators. Their effectiveness is bound up with your leadership qualities, their competencies and attitudes and how well you and they have done the preparation work of the first stages.

Keep the team focused on completing the objective. Keep the openness going and look out for cliques. Continue to monitor performance even in areas where the team has not shown any diminution or change in its results. If you let this go you will find the team slipping back into storming mode or worse still drifting quickly into the next recognized phase of team performance – boring.

Stage of development: boring

Issues at this stage:

A team will sometimes encounter a boring phase when they have been together for some time and little has changed in what you or they are doing or how they are doing it. This can kill creativity as the team works along well-rutted routes. Members have by now stopped challenging the traditional thinking of the team.

The performance angle

You could try changing people's jobs to stave off ennui. This can work quite well as can adding a new challenge or a new direction. We have seen successful project managers doing this in a way that does not seem to be reflecting the necessities of the project but the boring phase has dangers both in terms of a drop-off in performance and, of course, in losing people.

You almost certainly need an input from outside at this point, either brought into the team or brought in to help with a particular issue. As long, however, as the team is still focused on achieving the objectives of the project beware of introducing change for its own sake.

Stage of development: mourning

Issues at this stage:

It may not be your problem, but at the end of a project when a team is breaking up, some members will have a sense of personal loss. This is important to them and therefore to the organization. It is also extremely important to the team leader who is going to receive them into a new team. The mourning phase also happens if someone, particularly someone with a strong personality or a vital skill, leaves the team at any stage. Recognize the real danger that the team goes back to the forming and storming phases.

End the project with a bang not a whimper. Bring in as senior a member of the organization as you can get to come to the final celebration and thank the team for its efforts. Have a party but beware of inviting non-team members, such as spouses, because they lead the conversation in different directions and may cause the team not to focus on the purpose of the event, which is to part company in a social way and discuss where they are going next. In this regard it should be seen to by a team leader that all members know where they are going next so that the last tasks of the project are carried out in a positive atmosphere with the team looking forward to their next role.

Summarising these phases in team development, the role of the team leader is to move the team through to the performing stage as quickly and effectively as possible and *keep them there*.

Notes

1   Alan Bennett (1998) *Writing Home*, Faber and Faber.

Section 5

KEEPING COUNT

Introduction

Have you ever tried to argue with a finance director? They don't play fair. They have at their disposal an army of jargon, calculated to wrong-foot any up and coming manager. Take managers promoted into facing new challenges. They are trained for the physical task they have been assigned, but have no experience of the bunch of financial hurdles and measures that come with the job.

Much of this financial information they feel they ought to know since they probably learnt the basics at college. Or perhaps they are finding it difficult to make the bridge from the basics at college to the real world of business they find themselves in. Another thing – they would actually understand some of this financial information if it were expressed differently, using the same language they had been taught. It all appears to be a distraction from the job they want to do rather than a help to getting it done.

But it's a vicious circle. If you ignore the financial side of your job you will start to lose control of the physical task. If you get behind with the administration it's only going to get worse. If you do not query figures which appear to be wrong, particularly cross-charges coming in from other parts of the business, you could find yourself carrying a huge load of costs dumped on you by someone who knows their way around the system, and has seen you coming. Even if there is no one in your organization with such evil intent, you must not rely on the internal costing systems, as they are very difficult to get right and are notoriously inaccurate. The difficulty is making the systems keep up with changes in the organization.

If this last fact surprises you, you probably need to refresh yourself on the difference between financial accounts, the ones they publish, and management accounts, which are meant to assist everyone to run the business and meet their objectives.

The point in the end, of course, concerns decision-making. You can make a decision that seems correct for the organization but is financially wrong and vice versa. The aim here is to combine your functional skills with knowledge of the financial consequences of your decisions. If you can do this you are on the way to being a more effective manager.

Question 30   *How do I impress upon my people the importance of protecting and improving profit margins?*

Here are two salutary tales of two middle managers with opposing views of how to manage a profit and loss account. Use them as examples to build your own picture of the margins in your business and get your people to understand the critical nature of margins.

Sally Cranfield is an account manager at Compusell, a supplier of computer solutions, and she has a problem. Sally's job is to increase sales of computer products and services to her accounts. She has to do it profitably but the important measures she works towards are orders and deliveries or revenue. This is made more significant by the fact that the salespeople under her are targeted solely on orders. This brings her under huge pressure to make each proposal they put in front of customers as competitive as possible, particularly in terms of price.

Here is the estimated profit and loss account for a deal in which her people are involved.

Table 5.1   Sally's profit and loss account.

	No of units	Price per unit	Total
Sales	100	£10	£1000
Variable costs	100	£6	£600
Fixed costs			£300
Profit			£100

The salesperson involved in the sale gives her one problem, production give her another and administration a third. The customer, she is informed by the salesperson, wants to buy from Compusell, but has a cheaper offer from a competitor. He thinks that if Sally could knock just 2% off the price per unit, the purchaser can take a case for buying from Compusell to his board. That discount plus reducing the order to only 98 units will make the customer's budget work.

Management has agreed with the production department to a slight increase in the price of the unit; it's only 2%, but in the circumstances she cannot pass this on to the customer.

Administration has been saying for some time that there would be a slight increase in their costs due to increased charges from the IT department. It's only 2%.

Sally knows that these four changes to the proposition are all against the interests of her profit and loss account, but the numbers seem small, the customer has a lot of clout, and the salesperson is going to miss his target if he does not get this order. She agrees to the changes.

Look at the actual damage this decision makes to the profit and loss account.

Table 5.2   Sally's revised profit and loss account.

	No of units	Price per unit	Total
Sales	98	£9.80	£960.40
Variable costs	98	£6.12	£599.76
Fixed costs			£306.00
Profit			£54.64

Each 2% adjustment, all to Sally's disadvantage, has combined to knock nearly 46% off the profit of this deal.

Over at HAR, a recruitment consultancy, Andy McRae, the new managing director, is also taking a number of seemingly small decisions aimed at starting the process of re-establishing falling profitability. His executives sell a package of material to clients to keep them up to date on matters to do with employment law.

A major HAR client is likely to buy 100 of these and Andy wonders if the executive could do better. 'I want everyone to sell just a few more of these,' he says to the executives. 'Get each client to take just 2% more copies even though we are increasing the selling price a little, by 2%.'

He buys the package from a printer/packager who, he convinces, should lower the cost to HAR just a fraction, just 2%.

He has also been working for a while on the administration function and has told them to find some economies. 'Every little helps,' he says. 'Just knock 2% off what you spend right now.'

Andy's starting point was exactly the same as Sally's but he has made the slight adjustments in his favour.

The deal to the major client now looks like this.

Table 5.3   Andy's profit and loss account.

	No of units	Price per unit	Total
Sales	102	£10.20	£1040.40
Variable costs	102	£5.88	£599.76
Fixed costs			£294.00
Profit			£146.64

When the 2% works in your favour the addition to the profit is over 46%. Andy's company went from strength to strength – but they never recruited Sally.

When you think that Compusell is doing similar deals all over the world you can see the huge difference these tiny adjustments make. And that is why you need to understand the detail. You will end up making some tough decisions, but the rule of 2% could work for you starting today.

The people angle

Ask yourself if your team is adequately aware of the financial side of business, and put in place some help. It may be a session with the finance department or the use of e-learning and remote coaching, but putting such training in place will certainly give you return by increasing the profitability of each team member's activities.

Question 31   *How do I look for the easiest and best ways to improve my profit margin?*

Increased customer expectations and competitor performance are driving the need to constantly review ways of increasing revenues or decreasing cost. Systematic margin analysis enables non-financial managers and teams to identify ways of improving business unit, product or service line profitability.

At each stage of the process these are the principles that you should bear in mind.

- Protecting and growing profit is the responsibility of everyone in the business – not just the financial director.
- A basic understanding of the factors that influence profit can result in people changing the way they do things for the benefit of the business.
- Profits can be improved by increasing revenues or by reducing costs.
- Revenues can be increased by increasing sales volumes or by increasing sales price.
- Costs can be reduced by reducing distribution costs, product costs, input costs (cost of supplies), process costs or overhead costs (fixed costs of production and management).

Increase revenues

Improve fit with the market
Can we change the design of our products and services to make them more attractive to our target markets?

Increase sales effort
Will more effort and resources in our sales force increase sales significantly?

Increase brand awareness
Should we improve the general awareness in the market place of our products, services and company?

Lower price
Will lowering the price significantly increase sales volumes?

Grow market
Can we grow the overall market size so maintaining the same market share will increase sales?

Grow segment
Can we increase the overall size of the segment we compete in?

Sell to new markets
Are there other markets that might buy our products and services?

Increase price
Will increasing the price generate additional unit margin without losing sales?

The process angle

Get teams to look at the opportunities for increasing revenues in each element of the business.

Reduce costs

Improve channel efficiency
Can we change our distribution or logistics chain to make the sales process more efficient?

Redesign products
Can we change the design of products and services to make them cheaper to make, buy or support?

Reduce product range
Will reducing the number of products made or sold reduce costs associated with complexity?

Reduce cost of supplies
Can we buy cheaper elsewhere?

Reduce supplies complexity
Can we reduce the number and complexity of the materials and inputs we buy in or consume?

Reduce supplier complexity
Can we reduce the total number of suppliers that we have to deal with?

Reduce inventory costs
Can we reduce the amount of stock and materials we hold whilst not adversely impacting on service levels?

Change workflow (processes)
Should we change the order in which tasks are done to make the process more efficient?

Improve quality
Can we reduce the amount of wastage or rework?

Automate
Will the use of technology make the process more efficient?

Improve skills levels
Will more or better training improve productivity?

Consolidate facilities
Can we reduce our overheads – fewer buildings and offices?

Consolidate equipment
Can we utilize our equipment more effectively?

Consolidate roles
Can we reduce the number of people required to perform the tasks?

Reduce finance charges
Can we structure our loans to reduce payments?

Key questions

When completing the analysis, here are the key questions that you should ask yourself for both areas – increasing revenues and reducing costs.

1   What actions are necessary to improve profitability in each element?
2   What is the relative impact of each improvement opportunity? Score them one to five where five represents dramatic impact on profit and one represents marginal impact on short-term profit.
3   What is the relative urgency for each improvement opportunity? Score them one to five where five means immediate action with a limited window of opportunity and one means it can be undertaken at any time.
4   Finally, what is the status of each area for improvement?
   • red – immediate action is required (high impact and urgency)
   • amber – future action is probably going to be required
   • green – no action required.

A formal analysis should be conducted as part of any planning process for all product markets. This may be completed on a regular basis (annually) or by exception whenever profit or cashflow problems are forecast.

The performance angle

Most managers' spend is dominated by people costs. Up to 80% of many budgets is for the salaries and ancillary costs of staff. This makes it inevitable that actions taken to reduce costs can appear rather trivial, like cancelling the free chocolate biscuits at the coffee machine or stopping people travelling business class. It may be helpful to make sure that people understand this, and that the alternative to these economies is to lose people. Remind them that profit improvement is everyone's responsibility.

Question 32   *How do you persuade the sales force not to give away discounts?*

'Sorry, mate, I've found a cheaper quote.' What does your sales force do when it hears these words? If they generally come straight back to managers asking for permission to give a discount, you have a problem. There is often a simple reason that salespeople do this – they do not understand how a small discount on the sales price produces an inordinately big impact on the bottom line.

The people angle

> *Build a similar model to table 5.1 for your business, and communicate it to your team.*

Take this example from the insurance industry and transfer it into a real example in your own line of business.

The insurance business has always been price sensitive. Intermediaries, and even consumers who can use the Internet, can trawl for the cheapest price. Table 5.4 graphically demonstrates the impact on the bottom line of giving away any of the commission percentage the broker earns from a sale.

Table 5.4   The impact on the bottom line.

	Before discount	After discount
Premium	£1000	£900
Cost of insurance	£800	£800
Gross margin	£200	£100
Expenses	£50	£50
Net profit	£150	£50

Here is a sale ruined by discounting commissions. The original commission rate is 20%. This gives the gross margin on £1000 as £200. Under pressure the salesperson gives a 10% discount. As a result the bottom line has decreased by 66%.

The process angle

> *Look at the paperwork the salespeople have to complete to register an order, and make sure it demonstrates to them the difference discounting makes.*

Question 33   *How do I compare the financial benefits of one possible project with another?*

In today's competitive environment, scarce resources must be deployed in a way that delivers maximum benefit to teams and to the business. Return on investment (RoI) calculation enables non-financial managers to critically

assess the potential value of an investment or project – balancing anticipated financial rewards with the appropriate risk profile.

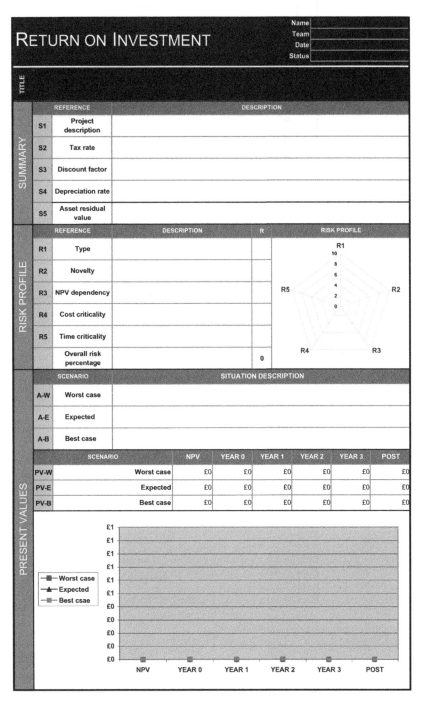

Fig. 5.1   Return on investment. (*Continued.*)

WORST CASE

FORECASTS	YEAR 0	YEAR 1	YEAR 2	YEAR 3	POST
B1 Cost reduction/avoidance					
B2 Revenue growth					
C1 Capital expenditure					
C2 Operating costs					
C3 Operating cashflow	£0	£0	£0	£0	
V1 Tax			£0	£0	£0
V2 Tax – capital allowances			£0	£0	£0
V3 Residual value				£0	
V4 Cashflow	£0	£0	£0	£0	£0
V5 Present value	£0	£0	£0	£0	£0
V6 Net present value (NPV)	£0				

EXPECTED

FORECASTS	YEAR 0	YEAR 1	YEAR 2	YEAR 3	POST
B1 Cost reduction/avoidance					
B2 Revenue growth					
C1 Capital expenditure					
C2 Operating costs					
C3 Operating cashflow	£0	£0	£0	£0	
V1 Tax			£0	£0	£0
V2 Tax – capital allowances			£0	£0	£0
V3 Residual value				£0	
V4 Cashflow	£0	£0	£0	£0	£0
V5 Present value	£0	£0	£0	£0	£0
V6 Net present value (NPV)	£0				

BEST CASE

FORECASTS	YEAR 0	YEAR 1	YEAR 2	YEAR 3	POST
B1 Cost reduction/avoidance					
B2 Revenue growth					
C1 Capital expenditure					
C2 Operating costs					
C3 Operating cashflow	£0	£0	£0	£0	
V1 Tax			£0	£0	£0
V2 Tax – capital allowances			£0	£0	£0
V3 Residual value				£0	
V4 Cashflow	£0	£0	£0	£0	£0
V5 Present value	£0	£0	£0	£0	£0
V6 Net present value (NPV)	£0				

Fig. 5.1   (*Continued.*)

The primary purpose of return on investment analysis is to get a simple financial indicator of the return on investment of a project, in order to compare one project to any other.

Using this return on investment model gives a consistent measure and makes sure that you are comparing like with like. The tool takes into account the relative riskiness of the project for comparison purposes. The tool also points out where extra effort should be concentrated so as to improve the likelihood that the financial objectives of the project are achieved. Using discounted cashflow techniques (see question 8 in section 2), the tool eventually reduces every project to a single number which can be used for comparison.

Summary

S1 Project description
This is a short description of the project.

S2 Tax rate
What is the marginal tax rate the tool should use for charging tax for increased profits and claiming allowances for expenditure? If you do not need to take tax into account, set this box to zero.

S3 Discount factor
What is the rate of return the project is required to exceed? This may be a standard for the organization. As long as a consistent rate is used the return on investment tool will make a relevant comparison amongst projects. You may have to revisit this after you have done a risk analysis on the project. Managers generally expect a high-risk project to offer a higher rate of return than a low-risk one. Take account of this when setting this 'hurdle' discount factor.

If inflation is at 3%, a positive net present value using a discount factor of 7% would be a low returning project, 12% a good return and anything over 20% an excellent return. Be careful, though: this rule of thumb is different for different industries.

S4 Depreciation rate
Enter the percentage annual depreciation rate. The tool uses this to calculate the tax cashflow. It allows tax against this depreciation rate in each of the three years of the project. The method the tool uses is kept simple but still provides a close approximation of the actual figures used in practice.

S5 Residual value percentage
At the end of three years some expenditure on capital items may have a residual value. What is the percentage residual value at the end of the three-year project analysis? If it will have no value, set this box to zero.

This figure is an estimate of the real residual value, and is independent of the depreciation rate used in S4. Your organization may have a rule for this.

Risk profile

R1 Type

What is the predominant type of benefit from this project – cost reduction (least risky), cost avoidance (middle risk) or revenue growth (most risky)?

When looking at the benefits of an investment, generally speaking there is much less risk in achieving cost reductions and cost avoidance than revenue growth. If the project is mainly concerned with cost reduction you should set the risk indicator, the next column, fairly low. If the benefits are mainly concerned with avoiding costs that would occur if this project were not implemented, mark the risk medium. If all the benefits are concerned with growing revenues, then it is a high-risk project and should be marked as such.

Each of these risks are set an indicator from one to ten, where one is very low risk and ten is extremely high.

R2 Novelty

How novel are the activities involved in carrying out this project?

- routine
- modification to existing project
- new type of project.

If the project is a repeat of things the organization has done many times before it is low risk. If the organization has operated in a similar way before then mark the risk as medium. If this project is entirely new, then mark the risk as high.

R3 NPV dependency

At what level of business case must this project give the appropriate NPV?

- must pass on worst case assumptions
- must pass on expected assumptions
- must pass on best case assumptions.

There are three levels of assumption in the tool if you choose to use them. Worst case assumptions describe the worst case in terms of the benefits. Expected are your best estimates of what is most likely actually to occur, and best case are the best you could hope for.

If there are also different levels of risk on costs, then do the two exercises separately. That is, take the expected level of benefits and compare it to the three levels of cost. Then take the expected level of cost and compare it against the three levels of benefits.

If the project is required to achieve its target NPV based on the worst case level of benefits mark the project low risk. If it is satisfactory to achieve the target NPV based on the expected level of benefits then mark it as medium risk, and if it can go ahead on the best case benefits mark it as high risk.

You may also combine the estimates. For example, if you combine the worst case costs and benefits you get the overall worst case.

R4 Cost criticality
How cost critical is the project?

- budgets are not important
- budgets are of normal importance
- budgets are very tight.

How critical is it that the project remains within its budget? If there is easy access to more funds mark it as low risk. If some more money could be made available mark it as medium. If there is absolutely no further money available mark it as high risk.

R5 Time criticality
How time critical is the project?

- timing is not important
- timing is of normal importance
- timing is a tight window of opportunity.

If there is plenty of slippage time available mark this as low risk. If it is important that this project is completed on time, then mark it medium. If there is a window of time available that must be achieved mark this as high risk.

Now calculate the overall percentage risk. If the overall percentage risk is around 50 you have a medium risk project, well above 50 is high and well below is low. If the risk is extreme in either direction you may care to review the discount factor that the project must beat.

Assumptions

Describe each of the three scenarios – A-W is worst case, A-E expected case and A-B best case. On what assumptions have you based the worst case scenario? Describe the possibilities here.

Present values

These represent the present value of the cashflows year by year for all cases. The total value, the single number that you can use for comparison is called the net present value or NPV. You calculate these values from the tables in the bottom part of the figure.

For each of the worst case, expected case and best case scenarios enter the following project financial data.

B1 Benefits – cost reduction and avoidance

What is the amount of cost that you are expending at the moment that will be saved through the implementation of this project? What costs that would occur if you do not implement this project would this project avoid?

B2 Benefits – revenue growth

What additional revenues will occur as a result of implementing this project?

C1 Cost

What capital expenditure does the implementation of this project require? You may find that there are specific rules in your organization to distinguish capital expenditure on this line from revenue expenditure on C2 in years 1, 2 and 3.

C2 Cost

What are the continuing running costs of this project?

C3 Operating cashflow

Calculate the year by year cashflow of this project

V1 Tax

Using the tax rate you gave at S2, charge tax on the benefits of the project and allow tax against revenue expenditure. If you have set S2 at 0, then ignore all tax considerations.

V2 Tax- capital allowances

Calculates tax allowances on capital expenditure as the capital value multiplied by the depreciation rate multiplied by the tax rate. You may have to check that this is relevant for your organization.

V3 Residual value

Calculates the residual value from the percentage you gave at S5 and puts this in as a positive cashflow item at year 3.

V4 Cashflow

This is the year by year cashflow of the project.

V5 Present value

This is the present value of the cashflows discounted by the factor you entered in S3.

V6 Net present value

This is a cross-addition of the present values to give the net present value. If this figure is positive it means that the project does meet the rate of return in S4. If it is negative it does not meet that rate.

The higher this number is, the better the return on investment. This is the single number you can use to compare one project with another financially.

Question 34   *How do people make money in low margin businesses?*

It is remarkable how managers in low margin businesses such as the packaged holiday business do so well. Partly it is simply practice, partly it is because they make changes carefully so that they always understand the impact that a change has on the bottom line and partly it is because they search for sidelines that offer much better margins than their core business.

The process angle

A little time ago a manager had to change the printer attached to his laptop. The main criterion was that its weight and bulk should allow him to carry it around easily. He remembered that the original one, which had eventually gone wrong, cost £200 some three years previously and was expecting a good reduction in price. In fact they were still the same price but for £200 you could now get a colour printer – quite impressive.

At the check-out he was given the hard sell by two assistants who tried to sell an extended warranty contract to cover years 2 and 3 of the printer's life. Being a sucker for a salesman he bought it. It cost £50 and was almost certainly where the retailer made the real money.

Similarly pubs, originally designed to make money out of drinks, now make the real profits from food. Packaged holiday companies have wafer thin margins on the holiday itself but do well out of selling holiday insurance. And so it goes on.

The principle is simple. Use the core business to cover your costs and make the cream on the top with other products that can be cross-sold.

Question 35   *What does hedging a risk mean in business terms?*

Most risks can be hedged. This means that in the event that one business risk goes against you, another will keep the wolf from the door.

The performance angle

There is a major parade taking place right through central London and some 25,000 people are expected to come to watch it. You have an opportunity to buy one of the concessions. If you buy the ice cream concession and it is a nice day you will clean up. If you buy the umbrella concession, you will make a fortune if it rains.

There is an alternative to this high risk/high return decision. You could go in with someone else and effectively own half of each concession. You are bound to make money, but nothing like the fortune you would have made had climatic conditions suited you. You pays your money and you takes your risks.

Question 36   *How do I remind myself of the meaning of financial terms and jargon?*

Glossary of financial terms and jargon

Accounting concepts   The basic assumptions underlying the preparation of accounts, namely going concern, accruals, consistency and prudence.

Accounting policies   The specific accounting bases judged by the business to be most appropriate to its circumstances and therefore adopted in the preparation of its accounts. For example, of the various methods of accounting for depreciation, the policy adopted may be to depreciate plant over a five-year period on a straight-line basis.

Accounts payable   American terminology for creditors.

Accounts receivable   American terminology for debtors.

Accrual   An expense or a proportion thereof not invoiced prior to the balance sheet date but included in the accounts – sometimes on an estimated basis.

Accruals concept   Income and expenses are recognized in the period in which they are earned or incurred, rather than the period in which they happen to be received or paid.

Advance corporation   The tax a company is required to pay (at the basic income tax rate) when it makes a distribution. The amount paid can subsequently be set off against the company's corporation tax liability for that year.

Asset   Any property or rights owned by the company that have a monetary value. Recently in some circumstances, assets have been included in company balance sheets if the company controls the asset without necessarily owning it, e.g. an asset on a finance lease.

Balance sheet   A statement describing what a business owns and owes at a particular date.

Borrowing ratio   This ratio is important in determining the credit worthiness of the business. It is defined as total debt (short-term and long-term loans) expressed as a ratio of shareholders' funds less intangible assets.

Capital employed   The aggregate amount of long-term funds invested in or lent to the business and used by it in carrying out its operation.

Cashflow   A statement of future, anticipated cash balances based on estimated cash inflows and outflows over a given period.

Consistency concept   The requirement that once an accounting policy for a particular item in the accounts has been adopted the same policy should be used from one period to the next. Any change in policy must be fully disclosed.

Cost of goods sold/Cost of sales   Those costs (usually raw materials, labour and production overheads) directly attributable to goods that have been sold. The difference between sales and cost of goods sold is gross profit.

Creditors   Those who have supplied goods or services to the business.

Current asset   An asset which, if not already in cash form, is expected to be converted into cash within twelve months of the balance sheet date.

Current cost   The convention by which assets are valued at the cost of replacement at the balance sheet date (net of depreciation for fixed assets).

Current liability   An amount owed which will have to be paid within twelve months of the balance sheet date.

Current ratio   The ratio of current assets to current liabilities in a balance sheet, providing a measure of business liquidity.

Debentures   Long-term loans, usually secured on the company's assets.

Debtors   Customers to whom goods or services have been sold but for which they have not yet paid.

Deferred asset/liability   An amount receivable or payable more than twelve months after the balance sheet date.

Deferred taxation   An estimate of a tax liability payable at some estimated future date, resulting from timing differences in the taxation and accounting treatment of certain items of income and expenditure.

Depreciation   An estimate of the proportion of the cost of a fixed asset that has been consumed (whether through use, obsolescence or the passage of time) during the accounting period.

Distribution   The amount distributed to shareholders out of the profits of the company, usually in the form of a cash dividend.

Dividend cover   The ratio of the amount of profit reported for the year to the amount distributed.

Dividend yield   The ratio of the amount of dividend per share to the market share price of a listed company.

Earnings per share   The amount of profit (after tax, but before any extraordinary items) attributable to shareholders divided by the number of ordinary shares in issue.

Equity gearing   This ratio shows the company's total exposure to debt. It is defined as shareholders' funds expressed as a ratio of total liabilities. It is of particular interest to unsecured creditors.

Exceptional item   Income or expenditure that, although arising from the ordinary course of business, is of such unusual size or incidence that it needs to be disclosed separately.

Expense   A cost incurred, or a proportion of a cost, the benefit of which is wholly used up in the earning of the revenue for a particular accounting period.

Extraordinary item   Material income or expenditure arising from outside the ordinary course of business and as such not expected to recur frequently or regularly. It needs to be disclosed separately.

Fixed asset   Asset held for use by the business rather than for sale.

Fixed cost   A cost that does not vary in proportion to changes in the scale of operations, e.g. rent.

Gearing   Gearing is the word used to describe the financing of the company in terms of the proportion of capital provided by shareholders (equity) compared with the proportion provided by loan capital (debt).

Gearing ratios   There are many different ways to measure gearing. The commonest is probably the ratio of debt to equity. That is the ratio of long-term loans to shareholders' funds. This can be measured in terms of nominal value or market value. Another common approach is to calculate the percentage of debt to total capital (debt plus equity). See also the notes on borrowing ratio, equity gearing and income gearing.

Gross profit   The difference between sales and the cost of goods sold.

Historic cost convention   The convention by which assets are valued on the basis of the original cost of acquiring or producing them.

Income gearing   This ratio highlights the profits available to meet the company's interest payments. It is defined as interest paid expressed as a percentage of pre-interest pre-tax profit (EBIT). It is the reciprocal of interest cover.

Interest cover   The relationship between the amount of profit (before interest and before tax) and the amount of interest payable during a period.

Liability   An amount owed.

Liquidity   A term used to describe the cash resources of a business and its ability to meet its short-term obligations.

Listed investments   Investments the market price for which is quoted on a recognized Stock Exchange. They may therefore be traded on that Exchange.

Long-term liability   An amount payable more than twelve months after the balance sheet date.

Market price   The price of a quoted security for dealing in the open market.

Net assets   The amount of total assets less total liabilities.

Net book value   The cost (or valuation) of fixed assets less accumulated depreciation to date. Net book value bears no relationship to market value.

Net current assets   The amount of current assets less current liabilities.

Net realizable value   Amount at which an asset could be sold in its existing condition at the balance sheet date, after deducting any costs to be incurred in disposing of it.

Nominal value   The face value of a share or other security.

Overhead   Any expense, other than the direct cost of materials or labour involved in making a company's products.

Prepayment   The part of a cost which is carried forward as an asset in the balance sheet to be recognized as an expense in the ensuing period(s) in which the benefit will be derived from it, e.g. the payment in advance of rates.

Price/earnings ratio   The relationship between the market price of a share and its latest reported earnings per share.

Profit   The difference between the revenues earned in the period and the costs incurred in earning them. A number of alternative definitions are possible according to whether the figure is struck before or after tax, extraordinary items, distributions, etc.

Profit and loss   A statement summarising the revenues and the costs incurred in earning them during an accounting period.

Provision   The amount written-off in the current year's profit and loss account in respect of any known or estimated loss or liability. Strictly the term should only be used if the amount or timing is uncertain.

Quick ratio   The ratio of those current assets readily convertible into cash (usually current assets less stock) to current liabilities.

Revaluation reserve   The increase in value of a fixed asset as a result of a revaluation. This needs to be included in the balance sheet as part of shareholders' funds in order to make the balance sheet balance.

Revenue reserves   The accumulated amount of profit less losses, generated by the company since its incorporation and retained in it. It may be called by other names.

Revenue   Money received from selling the product of the business.

Share capital   Stated in the balance sheet at its nominal value and (if fully paid, and not subject to any share premium) representing the amount of money introduced into the company by its shareholders at the time the shares were issued.

Shareholders' funds   A measure of the shareholders' total interest in the company, represented by the total of share capital plus reserves.

Share premium   The surplus over and above nominal value received in consideration for the issue of shares.

Statement of standard accounting practice   Statements issued by the accountancy bodies that describe approved methods of accounting.

Tax credit   The amount of tax deducted at source (at the basic rate of income tax) by a company from any dividend payment.

Turnover   Revenue from sales.

Variable cost   A cost that increases or decreases in line with changes in the level of activity.

Working capital   Current assets less current liabilities, representing the amount a business needs to invest – and which is continually circulating – in order to finance its stock, debtors and work-in-progress.

Work-in-progress   Goods (or services) in the course of production (or provision) at the balance sheet date.

Section 6

DEALING WITH PEOPLE

Introduction

Implementing a plan is much easier if you have gathered the right team of people to do it. Hiring people may therefore be the most important thing that a manager does. People hire and manage people in many different styles. Some total dictators, performing like a nineteenth century mill owner, continue to get results even when they are vastly unpopular with their subordinates. In our experience most people like that don't make it much beyond middle management roles, but some do become the managing director and are frequently unsuccessful at that point because disgruntled employees have no form of recourse or appeal and therefore no loyalty. At best, such a person performs to target for a period of time, at worst the senior management team loses interest in the organization's objectives and just concentrates on not being beaten up. Unfortunately some exceptions prove this rule and some successful managers perform well with a team that hates to be there; but geniuses, even evil ones, make their own rules.

Let's imagine that you are not such a genius and that you agree with us that hiring and other stages in managing people are a constant search for a real win-win result.

Question 37　What concisely and precisely is a manager's job?

At some point every manager needs to show that they have thought about the job of a manager. Remember KISS: keep it simple, stupid. And get the level right, a mixture of pragmatic efficiency and wide-thinking talent. Here is a question for you. Who is responsible for achieving the business results of a team? If your answer was the manager, then you probably need to rethink the relationship between a manager and their team. Like it or not, it is the team that produces the results and managers at their best are enablers rather than performers.

Managers are there to enable their people to give their best.

- They are effective implementers of corporate and divisional strategy. They are always able to connect their activities with the bigger picture.

- As well as implementing it, they have a role in influencing high-level strategy. First line managers are the voice of their people, markets and suppliers. They see the changes day to day and are in the best position to question or suggest alterations to the way the organization goes about its affairs.

The performance angle

Some second line managers get somewhat disillusioned. They are a little way from the real action but not yet on the bridge. One I know, when asked to define his job, said: 'In this organization, I take material from my physical and electronic in-boxes and transfer it to my out-boxes. Sometimes I read it and add to it, and sometimes I don't bother. It doesn't seem to make any difference.'

- Managers are a skilled resource to their team. They must add value when they are in action helping the team. When a sales manager goes to see a customer, or a purchasing manager a supplier, for example, the plan must make them do or say something that could not be done or said by the team member. A good example is when a production manager visits a supplier and introduces the topic of the environment and other green issues.
- Managers know how the organization works and can thus add to the efficiency and productivity of their team.

Question 38   *How do I hire the right person into a team?*

The most important point in starting the hiring process is to have complete clarity on what the job is and what tasks you want the person to perform. In other words, start from roles and responsibilities. Don't rush this part of the process, and at some point in the interview process check your and the delegate's understanding of the role by asking them to give a presentation on what they believe the role is and the tasks are. Remember that selection is a two-way process. Just as you are looking for the right person, the candidate is looking for a job with the right fit for their skills and aspirations. They try to change the job from, say, 70% of what they are looking for to being all that they want. Compromise on this unless such development of the role is now or in the future going to lead the team in the wrong direction.

It is often true that the strategy of a candidate, that is their perception of how they will carry out the role, can look right but the detail look wrong. This is particularly true in the more senior roles where you are working with a much smaller pool of potential team members with the right skills and competencies. In this circumstance, go back to the purpose of the job and how it fits with the results you need.

Let's emphasize again the importance of getting recruitment right. Don't rush it, even if the requirement for the person is urgent. Stop, think and work at a sensible pace. You have to be brave and look at the situation in the same way as an experienced salesperson, whose view always is that if something feels wrong in a sales campaign, take action as though it is wrong. Similarly, if you have doubts about recruiting, then don't appoint.

Bringing key people into a team really needs to have the team involved in the recruitment process. During the assessment phase get all the key team members to meet the candidates, and give the candidates a chance to present to the team. A word of caution on this: only do it if the team is competent to recruit. Your human resources people should assess the candidate's ability to do the job; the team is helping to advise on how the individual will fit in. Don't ask lower levels of staff to make presentations if presentations have no part in their job spec and where nervousness might cover up an individual's ability to do a job.

One final point – watch the types of question you ask. You may feel it perfectly proper to ask if the candidate has ever been involved in an employment tribunal, for example, but it is illegal, as is any other question that may hint at any form of discrimination.

The people angle

If you feel that a systematic approach to the comparison of one person with another would give you a sounder basis for your decision, try the decision-making template from question 2.

Question 39   How do I recruit a key person in a small business?

A small business cannot afford to make poor hiring choices. Yet people have a bad habit of recruiting the first person that drifts by the door, who is willing to risk working for a small business. There are the usual paradoxes here.

1   You need to cast the net wide to make sure you get the right person; but this takes up your valuable time which should be spent selling and delivering.
2   Using professional help solves this problem and often gives you the best result; but the fee, frequently 33% of the first year's salary plus expenses, is a huge drain on a small business cashflow and a leg iron

for the candidate targeted to become cash positive in as short a time as possible.

3   When you are recruiting someone from a big company, you may have to paint an optimistic picture of potential results and the joys of working for a small business. But, particularly in a start-up, you are not in a strong position to forecast let alone guarantee that they will achieve those results or enjoy the stresses and strains of a business in which the cashflow is continuously problematic. The old maxim holds – try to under-promise and over-perform.

Question 40   *Do I really have to check on references?*

In theory your recruitment process should be capable of standing alone in assessing whether or not an individual has the competencies to do the job. This leads many people not to bother checking references with former employers or asking for evidence of qualifications. But if you look for occasions when a person has looked ideally fit to do the job, but has proved to work in a way that causes difficulty to the team leader or other people in the organization, you will find myriad examples. Check references to discuss the conduct of a person rather than their competency to do the job.

Listen carefully to the replies. Most people are kind to people leaving their employment even, frankly, if they are delighted to see the back of them. Indeed some unscrupulous managers will give glowing references as a device to get rid of the awkward squad. (Be careful about doing this yourself, as you can open yourself up to litigation from either party.) Nevertheless, you can normally tell from the choice of words and the length of pauses before offering a response to questions how sincere the person is being. Read between the lines.

The other reason for taking up references and checking on qualifications is to avoid fraudulent conduct. If the person is claiming professional qualifications needed to do the job, you must check these although, admittedly, the number of rogue anaesthetists is going to be small.

Question 41   *Is there an easy way to fire people?*

The quick answer to this question is no. Even very senior people are known to take a very large brandy before carrying out the final interview of the dismissal process.

The process angle

Remember, firing people is a process. Dismissing is not the first action. In a large company your human resources people will guide you step-by-step through the sequence that explains the non-performance problems of a member of staff, gives

them the opportunity to add to their skills or change their attitude in order to per-
form to specification and, perhaps most importantly, understand how and why they
do not fit the role they are in at the moment.

Here is some advice from Fiona Green, the Chief Executive Officer of a National Health Service Trust, talking about the first interview in the process with a member of staff who has a performance problem.

'Get the news out immediately, and then go into support mode. Go over the administration and be precise about the timing and the sequence of events. It is not just emotionally important, it is also legally important to take every care not to strip away a person's dignity. Sit them down, take the reaction and stay with them.'

In any case, but particularly in the case of redundancy, you need to make it clear that they have some choices in, for example, timing and in how they want to work with their team.

Let's assume you have gone through the process and the member of staff has been unable or unwilling to change their behaviour and perform to specification. Since the whole process takes at least three but up to six months, it's actually quite bad luck if they are still there. Many people use the period of the dismissal process to find a more suitable job.

The people angle

The human resources manager needs to think about the competence of the firing manager. Some people are too nice to handle the dismissal process, while others get too bogged down with the administration of the dismissal and lose sight of their other responsibility which is to the person being dismissed. Many managers in this regard react prematurely if you tell them to think about the dismissal option too early.

The overall message to the human resources manager is – can you hold up what you have done to tribunal scrutiny?

The process angle

This is no time to be anything except process-driven. This is a complex minefield. Be rigorous in agreeing the requirement of the job and making sure that they under-stand as accurately as possible the performance problem. The very act of writing this down helps both parties to be specific. Don't tease. It is bad practice to have made up your mind to dismiss no matter how hard the person being dismissed tries to modify their behaviour. Remember that it is your job to work with people who perform to specification, not to work with people that you like.

Plan the hierarchy of getting the bad news across. Start from a softly, softly approach, showing a positive attitude to assist the person to improve performance. Then move to becoming more specific, as in stating that if there is no improvement, disciplinary procedures will start. Once again, the overall message to managers is that they must not be half-hearted about this process and that they must be prepared to change their mind.

However, let's assume that you have a member of staff who has stuck at it through the whole process and you have to go through performance dismissal. Your aim is to move to a discussion as quickly as possible as to where the person might specifically go, how they should take control or generally what their new direction might be. However, don't get into such a discussion until they have completely accepted that they are going.

OK, that's dismissing someone in a nutshell. Don't forget as you go through the tortuous process, however, that the person with the problem is on the other side of the desk, not yours, even if you need a large brandy to remind yourself of this.

Question 42   How do I maintain the 'buzziness' of a happy team?

It is a truth, unfortunately, that very successful teams are easier in this regard than teams struggling with a number of things going wrong. Nevertheless, talking to human resources people, you can get a series of tips on maintaining that feeling of comfort and enthusiasm that emerges when a team is working well together.

First of all be rigorous in spotting where growth is going to come and changing the team's focus and resource allocation to meet the expected change. An enthusiastic team will lose its buzziness when some of its members appear overloaded and the allocation of tasks seems unbalanced. In the end an overly heavy workload turns people off. At best it makes them operate grudgingly and at worst results in the loss of key people.

Talk a lot with the team about how it is functioning. Make sure that you identify the team's strengths as well as its weaknesses. After all it is its strengths that you are trying to transfer to other people, particularly new people. Get them to talk about themselves and work out why the team is blending well.

The people angle

It is good practice to expand the usefulness of brainstorming sessions by asking a sub-set of the team to prepare for a particular topic. Then bring them together and agree a team approach with actions on the appropriate members. Margin analysis, question 31, is a good example of this, if you ask sub-sets of the team to look at different aspects of revenues and costs.

Talk about the team's values and principles. Indeed the best teams build some basic beliefs into their business plan. Maintaining the style of a team is most difficult when things need to change. At that point the documentation of values and beliefs is useful in making sure you don't throw the baby out with the bath water. If the value or belief collapses in the new situation then your analysis of the fundamental strengths of the team was not rigorous enough.

One senior human resources manager we talked to believes that you can build the capacity for planning changes into the team's style by regularly discussing where you are and what you are like, and working out what you need to be like. In the end the most powerful organizations can tailor themselves to the individual through their identification with a team.

Question 43   *How do you keep staff in a seller's market?*

This is a hard question and managers need to implement the answer before the seller's market arrives. The overarching responsibility of the team manager is demonstrating strong and fair leadership. Having said that, you have to get the hygiene right in terms of pay, terms and conditions. If the circumstances of your organization are that you cannot compete with the rest of the market then look for what else you can offer. Good people will, for example, settle for a lower salary if they are sure that their training and development needs are going to be seriously considered with time and resources allocated to it. They also enjoy working with colleagues in a team which has a style they can identify with. People want to see everyone in the team valued. This means that more administrative people such as secretaries should be involved in the team – perhaps more than their task, on the face of it, requires.

People also look for organizations that do not believe that the only good member of the team is one that puts the organization before everything. Demonstrate therefore that you take the work/life balance seriously and encourage people to schedule their time off as well as their work diary. Take an interest in what they do when they are not at work and in their families. Opinion is divided on the involvement of partners and children in the social activity of the team. The good manager respects that difference of opinion by making it possible for people to join in family events but perfectly allowable for those who do not wish to do so to miss out on it.

Fiona Green, the Chief Executive Officer of a National Health Service Trust, believes that the involvement of spouses offers more problems than it does benefits.

Question 44   **How do you decide whether to hire from outside or promote from within?**

Teams clearly prefer an ethos that includes wherever possible promoting from within. This can give you problems when a job that someone is leaving is itself hard to fill. Nevertheless the ethos that you develop among your people is, overall, more important than those particular situations.

Having said that, you must not compromise. Remember that you are succeeding through having people with the skills and motivation to carry out their jobs. This means that you must go outside if there is no completely suitable candidate within. It is wise to show that you have tried for an internal candidate. It is also wise to make public the definition of a different job that clearly demonstrates the requirements for different skills; so you have to go outside.

The exception to all of this is diversification of the team into an area of activity, be it in product or market, completely new to it. An internal manager in such a situation will almost certainly add to the already considerable problems of a diversification if they are doing the job and learning from scratch at the same time. Much better is to bring someone in with experience of the new area.

Question 45   **How do you prevent people working too long hours?**

If someone gets the work/life balance wrong they will eventually, for whatever reason, perform less well or suffer health problems. It is in their and the team's interest therefore that you interfere and help them to get the balance right. Many managers believe that after, say, 18 months in a new job, a team member should by definition be competent to do it in the contracted hours allowed.

Encourage this type of thinking. As usual your example and leadership will be key to this. People notice, for example, if you have sent them an e-mail at 8 o'clock at night or 6 o'clock in the morning; so you should avoid this.

The people angle

'Prioritize business and family life. Business is for a maximum of 40 years; family is for life.'

Peter G Birch, Chairman, Land Securities

Question 46   *How do you prevent an ageing founder member hindering a company's progress?*

In many small businesses, the founder member frankly overstays their welcome. There can come a situation where their resistance to change in the way the company does business, and their resistance to new methods, for example to the introduction of technology, can threaten the growth of the business in a changing product/market environment. This is not an easy one to solve.

In talking to two people who have survived the problem, this seems to be the best advice.

Try to get the founder's agreement to doing a team analysis, such as agreeing on the strengths, weaknesses, opportunities and threats to the business. This should demonstrate to their satisfaction that change is necessary and that you are going to carry it through.

Insist on the expenditure on technology where necessary; but find some way of allowing the founder to work without it even if you have to do some duplication of effort to make this possible.

Finally, admit defeat and try to get them to limit their activities to areas, for example with old customers similarly resistant to change, where they can do least harm. If you have offices in other places, particularly abroad, encourage them to go on visits, and introduce change in their absence. Don't forget in this case the need to allow them to continue as normal, or they will try and undo the progress you have made.

Section 7

MANAGING YOUR CAREER

Introduction

Not all of the most frequently asked business questions stem from eagerness to learn and develop new skills and techniques. Some are more blatantly about an individual's career and how to avoid the pitfalls and political minefields of corporate life. So we felt that we had to include some questions on this theme.

We also asked several senior managers for their tips in this regard, and were delighted with the replies that many of them made. Here they are collected into a sort of section of career wisdom, some to do with performance, some with process and a lot with people.

Question 47　*How would you summarize how to make it to the top?*

We asked a number of senior managers for their concise answer to this question, and perhaps Murray Stuart hit the nail on the head most economically.

The process angle

He introduced us to the four Cs, a chairman's thoughts on making it to the top.

1　*Wherever you are, well honed* **Communication** *skills are highly important.*
2　**Continued learning** *– lifelong learning is no longer a buzzword but a real necessity to be conscientiously practised.*
3　**Confidence** *in yourself – never be afraid to seize sensible opportunities – be ambitious.*
4　**Care**, *and attention to those you love and indeed to those you work with. A selfish, narrow life soon becomes too difficult to correct.*

Murray Stuart CBE, Chairman, Scottish Power

Here are two other answers that are more about career and structure than self-development.

The performance angle

Henry Lewis was the Chief Executive Officer of Marks & Spencer. When asked why, out of all the management trainees that he joined with, he had made it right to the top, he said, 'You know, I really have no idea'. After some thought he added, 'But I have noticed that every job I have ever done has been abolished after I left it.'

This profound observation has good reason behind it. Many jobs exist because they have always done so rather than because they represent the best way of doing things. If someone goes into the job and does things the right way, they are probably going outside the original job description that set the post up in the first place. This changed way of operating gets results, but when the person who made the change leaves, his or her boss will have to change the structure and job description so that the new post consolidates the new way of working. The lesson here is to use your influence and authority to get the best results possible without paying much attention to how things were done in the past.

The corollary of abolishing your job is also true. Managers who succeed are the ones who help the organization keep up to date and who help to prevent it ossifying.

It is easier to create a new job if the change will help the organization achieve its objectives better, and it serves your own career purposes as well. Possibly starting from putting up an unsolicited paper or report, the creation of a new job falls into two parts. First formulate the changed way of doing business that will ensure that the job will exist. Sell this first. That is, show what the changes will do in business terms rather than in structural or people terms. If you reveal your hand at this stage there is a good chance that you are mistiming it by being too early. Don't give anyone the opportunity to say that what you are doing is for your own greater glory rather than the advancement of the organization. Having sold the change, produce your implementation plan and, of course, include the new positions required. Do not at this stage play any kind of shrinking violet game; clearly show that you are the person for the role you have chosen and defined. You have the business benefits behind you and they have been agreed, so tell people that you should have the job. Make sure the new job description has all the elements needed for the next step – access to senior management and a high profile when required. The risk and return on this career procedure will be very good if you have got it right. After all, you have moulded a job in which the circumstances and your skills will be a perfect fit.

The performance angle

> *A president of RCA is reported to have answered the question 'Why, when so many were called, were you chosen?' with the opposite of Henry Lewis's remark. He also purported not to know but said, 'I have noticed that no job I ever did existed before I got it.'*

The third and fourth answers are ever so simple.

The performance angle

> *Sir John Collins, the Chairman of National Power, puts it like this:*
> *'Agree annual objectives and targets with your line manager and ensure that your delivery exceeds expectations. In other words, perform as advertised.'*
> *Sir George Bull, Chairman of J Sainsbury, put it like this:*
> *'Study your subject well; observe carefully your customer requirements; strive mightily to fulfil that customer need and work hard and diligently at all times.'*

Question 48   *How much information do senior managers want in a report?*

Most managers err hugely on the side of putting too much information and detail into reports. Ken knows one senior manager who started in a new job by saying that any communication sent to him should be no more than one page long. Even with such a specific instruction most managers served up much more, and were astounded when they found that he had not read beyond page one. Don't forget the salesman's mantra: 'The only way you can be certain that a person is interested in what you are saying is if you are responding to their question.'

The process angle

> *'Keep your executive summaries short and snappy. If you need to pass the weight test, put it in the appendices. That will keep the jobsworths happy but won't detain the people you really want to notice your talents. Remember, you are trying to impress someone above you. He or she did not get where they are today by spending self-enhancement time on verbiage from a junior, some ambitious little swot's worthy but tedious magnum opus. By definition their time is in short supply; it is valuable to them. They have lunch to drink, golf to play and, even more important, people to impress. Actually, if they are not like that, you've got a problem. They will be no use*

to you and your career. If your boss is into detail treat him or her as a roadblock to your career and take avoiding action.'

Richard Humphreys, serial chairman

Question 49 How do you make yourself do the least attractive part of your job?

The people angle

'Always do unpleasant jobs at the earliest opportunity but do plan carefully how to execute them. There is nothing more distracting than having an unpleasant job hanging over you. They seldom turn out to be as nasty as you anticipate and there is always a sense of relief having completed an unpleasant job.'

George Paul, Chairman, Norwich Union

Question 50 How reliant on you should you make your boss?

The people angle

'Think carefully how you can make your boss's life easier. There is always a risk that your boss may come to rely upon you so much that he or she is reluctant to recommend you for promotion; but that is a risk worth taking in the quest to raise your profile in your boss's estimate.'

George Paul, Chairman, Norwich Union

Question 51 Should I take the appraisal system seriously?

From both your and your organization's point of view the answer to this question has to be yes. We have seen how the implementation of a plan is highly dependent on identifying and filling the skills and competency gaps of the people involved. The key to this is a close linkage between the appraisal system and everyone's personal development plan. Here is the view of one senior manager.

The people angle

'People have different aspirations, capability and motivation informing their decisions about career development. In recognition of this, the best advice to help individuals build a future that meets their needs is to "know yourself". In Natwest, we provide a considerable amount of support to our staff through the use of appraisal and development systems, psychometric testing, development centres and other technologies to help them develop this understanding. Equipped with this knowledge they are better placed to make decisions about what is right for them.'

Chris Wathen, Director of Human Resources, Natwest Group

Question 52   *When does being assertive look like being a troublemaker?*

Big companies do tend to look after managers who look after themselves. However, try not to take your selfish view of a situation as always your first starting point – it can become tedious even if what you are saying has merit. This involves taking a strategic look at your career, and sometimes sacrificing short-term advantage for long-term potential.

The people angle

'You might be better off doing an extra few months at £20,000 a year rather than causing grief by bellyaching. The eventual return could be well worth it.'

£1-million-a-year adman

Question 53   *Is making effective presentations as important as people seem to believe?*

Nowadays, presentations are used to communicate around the business very frequently. As such they are both an opportunity and a threat. Think about them hard, and remember that the measure of a good presentation is simply: 'Did it achieve its objectives?'

If you have a natural talent for making presentations and you can enjoy them once the nervousness has worn off, you put yourself ahead of the crowd. In some company cultures, indeed, you are pretty much on a slow track if your presentation skills are poor or if you look scared witless at the end of the presentation as well as the beginning. At an early stage in your career volunteer to be the person who presents the results of a workshop, or makes a presentation on some new topic to the departmental meeting.

The process angle – Ken's story

I had no idea of how useful presentations were until this incident happened to me. In the dark ages of the seventies the business world was burdened with a new tax – Value Added Tax. I was a graduate trainee at the time and my boss, who sometimes found it difficult to think of constructive things for a rookie to do, asked if I could have a look at this VAT business and make a presentation of what it was about to the next area meeting. I got hold of Government papers and found the concept of the tax hard to understand. I persevered and spoke to a load of people including Government people who were very helpful. At last I was able to understand how the tax worked in my terms. These were, of course, the terms that my colleagues in the area would also use. A bit of luck had me hear a joke on the radio about VAT inspectors being called Vatman and Robin, so I nicked that and used it as a running gag through the presentation. It went well and I knew that it had done my career no harm at all. My boss mentioned that it had gone well to his boss who told him that he had attended a presentation by some accountants on the tax and that no one in the audience had understood a word of it. I was asked to give the same presentation to the management team at my boss's boss's team meeting – very useful, high profile stuff.

If you are not a natural at this game, go on training until you can at least survive, although I do know one senior manager who made it to the top and remained a complete liability on his feet. When asked how he did it he replied, 'Ducking and weaving, old boy, I avoided the things like the plague.'

Funnily enough the usual suspects are the best tips for making effective presentations. Set tight objectives and talk exclusively in the terms of the audience. Try not to talk to mixed audiences. It can be difficult to make the same presentation to the marketing people and the research and development people at the same time even if the topic is of mutual interest.

It is a very good idea to announce the objectives at the start of the presentation. The audience then knows where you are going to take them. Some people avoid this since you do run the risk that someone in the audience will say that it will not be possible for you to achieve your objectives. Logically it is better to know this at the start of the presentation than at the end. Who knows? If you know what the audience's objections are you may be able to use the presentation itself to overcome them.

The process angle

Presentations are about them, the audience, rather than you, the speaker. It actually makes you look better when you are talking about them.

Think about your preparation in three areas – the structure of the content or argument, the mechanics of the room and the visual aids, and your personal delivery.

Question 54   *What is the structure of an effective presentation?*

Before you start make sure that it is the right time to make the presentation in the first place. Quite often you could achieve your objectives in some other way that costs less and possibly has less risk. Mind you, if the point of the presentation is to raise your profile then ignore this advice. Make sure also that you have done everything possible before the presentation that can help to achieve the objectives. Getting the most senior person on your side before you begin is a good idea. Finally make sure you know your audience well enough. What will motivate them to think your idea a good one? What is in it for them? Aim at making effective presentations as well as elegant ones and use your performance on the day to give it a theatrical edge.

Now prepare the background to the presentation. Who asked you to do this? Whom have you talked to, and who has helped you? Cover also whose agreement you already have to what you are proposing. The audience should now be aware of how well qualified you are to talk to them on this topic. Always ride your luck, in presentations, as in all aspects of your career. If a point has gone down well, consider if you need to work on that one and drop some other points that you have prepared.

Now state the problem or opportunity that you are addressing. You are there to agree that you and your audience have a problem and you have the solution, or that they have an opportunity and you know how to exploit it. If it is difficult to express your purpose as a problem or opportunity then you have not set your objective specifically enough.

Now comes the clever bit of preparation that will set your work ahead of the crowd. Get the audience to understand, and if possible agree the 'basis of decision' that they should use in looking at your solution. This is a much more subtle way of selling an idea than banging on about the features of your solution. The basis of decision you suggest will, of course, describe your solution. You are then able at a later time to say simply, 'And my suggested action plan meets the basis of decision we spoke about (or agreed) at the beginning of this session.' The more interactive you keep this part, and the more it appears that they have built their own basis of decision, the more likely you are to get their agreement.

Now reveal your solution. Do it in their terms, illustrate it with examples and make sure that at the end of this section the audience will be able to describe exactly how things will be if they adopt your idea.

The process angle

Be open to new ideas. Even if you have spent a lot of time preparing a presentation, you should still listen to your audience and be ready to accept an alternative idea if it is better than yours.

Now hit them with the benefits. These are the business and personal benefits they will get from your proposal. Now they should know what is in it for them.

If you are presenting to a customer or prospect, don't mistime the delivery of the section on why they should do business with your particular company. No one is in the least bit interested in your company unless they have provisionally decided that they want to adopt your solution. I am therefore convinced that you should never do the 'Why my company?' fanfare until someone in the audience has asked, 'Why should we go with you on this one?' or words to that effect. Similarly it is good technique to ask the enquirer what they would like to know about your organization, even if you have a well-prepared pitch. This helps you to tailor your pitch to what the audience thinks is important rather than what you think is important. Sorry to bang on, but we have seen more presentations ruined by overselling the presenter's company at the wrong time than by any other misdemeanour.

The time has come to close for agreement. Make sure you can spell out the next one or two steps that need to be carried out to make progress. If they agree to your future plan they have agreed with your suggestion.

Question 55   *How do you organize the logistics of an effective presentation?*

More can go wrong with the mechanics or logistics of a presentation than you would believe. We have seen people arrive with visual aids that the room did not have the facilities to show. We have seen piles of overhead projector slides dropped and mixed up, flipchart stands falling over, overhead projector slides slowly curling up until they display nothing and so on. The main messages here are – keep it simple, know the room and rehearse in it beforehand if possible.

Next get the timing right. People do not like presentations going on beyond the time allowed, particularly if you are one item on an agenda. Plan your timing to get to the future plan well before the end of the time allocated. Three quarters of the way through is perfect, since you then have time to deal with questions and objections. No audience likes to be told to keep their questions to the end. Why should they? If they need an answer to follow your drift they need to ask the question.

If there is more than one speaker at the same meeting there are some further hazards, which is why many people prefer to work on their own. Make sure every speaker has compared notes, and that they are all there for the whole presentation. An audience loves nothing more than one speaker contradicting something a previous speaker said.

Be prepared for the questions you will be asked and objections that will be raised. It is excellent technique to role-play the audience's questions with a colleague at rehearsal time. You will find that you have practised eighty per cent of the questions if you do, and will produce much smoother and more convincing answers as a result. If someone asks a silly question, the rest of the audience will be aware of this and laugh, outwardly or inwardly, at his or her foolishness. Don't add to their discomfort by scoring a witty point off their stupidity. Funnily enough, this brings the audience back on to the questioner's side and makes them regard you as the sort of person who kicks a person when they are down.

Finally, rehearsal is not optional. If you rush in to give the usual pitch to a new audience without thinking it through and rehearsing, it will look exactly as though that is what you have done.

Presentations have great potential to give good return to the careerist, but as usual they carry the consequent risk. Most of this risk is in the mechanics of the event.

The process angle

'If I have to pick just two pieces of advice for business presentations, I would say, "Rehearsal with the role-playing of the question and answer session, and the use of visual aids that are pictures rather than words or figures."'

Anthony Jay, creator of Yes, Minister

Question 56   *How do you deliver an effective presentation?*

Strange as it may seem, if you set good objectives and get the structure and mechanics right, your delivery will not be the make or break of the presentation. This is why many people who do not regard themselves as natural performers can give effective presentations time after time. If you are using the right words in the right order and your visual aids work, most of the battle is done. But there are some rules of thumb that can be useful.

The process angle

> *'Polish your presentation skills. Everything can be learned, and we live in a superficial world. So make sure you are superficially good. You are more likely to make impact with style rather than substance.'*
>
> Richard Humphreys, serial chairman

The first of these is to check that the talk is interesting. That means really interesting to the audience not just to you. This rule tends to make presentations shorter rather than longer. The old comic's maxim 'always leave them wanting more' holds good in business life. Do not go on if you have achieved your objective. Just because you have prepared another five slides you do not have to use them. Some people regularly unsell an idea by going on after they had received agreement to their proposition.

Use spoken rather than written English and try to vary your voice. If you have a tendency to be monotonous, use more than one type of visual aid to gain variety. Move around; sit down from time to time; do anything to keep the audience's attention.

Making the audience laugh is a good thing; telling jokes in the manner of 'I wonder if you have heard the one about…' is bad. Always weave yourself into the story. You met the person who said… or you were in the train with a man who… Even if it is an outrageous gag that you could not possibly have witnessed, they will enjoy the story much more than if you raise a huge sign post saying, 'joke coming'.

Finally check your delivery for the abstract and avoid it. Talk in simple concrete terms and don't pad it out in any way. Avoid the slow track of poor presenters by following these simple rules of persuasive communication.

Question 57   *Is there a career version of 'managing by wandering around'?*

'Managing by wandering around' was a management slogan in Hewlett Packard for many of its most successful years. It simply emphasized the informal approach which management should make to their people and other teams by wandering around. It enabled managers to know what was happening at the grass roots and gave very short chain of command feedback from, for example, the customer base. It was best exemplified in the canteen where everyone regardless of rank had lunch. This even included customers. The only difference between a customer table and a normal table was that they served wine to customers. For salespeople this was a golden opportunity and they frequently could introduce any old customer to a passing senior manager.

The career equivalent is stated here by Richard Humphreys.

The people angle

'There is no stronger way of building a career than working the corridors.' Richard, in his normal practical, if not cynical, way, adds a note of caution about whom you meet in the corridors. 'It is all very well being loyal and supportive to a friend who is struggling or who is incompetent and uncharismatic. But don't do it in a way that reflects on you. Give them real and meaningful support, but surreptitiously. Avoid being tarred with their brush.'

Question 58   *How do you find a good time to do training?*

It is not uncommon for training to be cancelled at little or no notice. What happens is that the person booked on the course, or more frequently their manager, decides that there are a number of critical tasks that need to be done during the training period. Since that manager may never appreciate the value of the skills learnt in training they continue to cancel willy-nilly. This is not good for the organization. First of all it costs money to cancel without notice. Secondly the training should be part of the personal development plan that is enabling the individual to perform the current task to standard or preparing them for their next job.

Crucially however it is not good for the individual. It smacks of being out of control and it ignores the advice of many senior managers including George Paul.

The people angle

'Always take every opportunity offered to receive training. Give careful thought to your training needs before any appraisal interview.'
George Paul, Chairman, Norwich Union

Question 59   *When is it right to be proactive in a team leader type job?*

Almost all the time. If you look at managers who have been in the same job for a number of years and whose career seems to have faltered you are probably looking at a classic reactor. They obey the rules, follow the business's processes and never suggest the need for change. Indeed they are probably near the front line of those who naturally oppose change. The organization's problem with them is that they are losing that individual's feedback from the market or the product line which should be informing it of the need for change.

The key is to look at what you are doing, decide whether it is wholly in the organization's interests and look for ways of suggesting and implementing improvement.

The performance angle

John Newbern put it as succinctly, but in three groups: 'Those who make things happen, those who watch things happen and those who ask, "What happened?"'

Question 60   When is it right in your career to take a risk without authority?

We have already seen the good advice to perform as advertised. However, the career-minded manager looks for opportunities to over-perform by grasping opportunities. The first example is brilliant in its glorious simplicity. It says that listening to other people, particularly people involved in a negotiation, will frequently give you opportunities to out-perform. We have already looked at the importance of listening in the sales environment; here it is in the world of negotiation.

The performance angle

'My way was to plan what I wanted, try to distract the quarry by conceding generously on minor points and hope the big ones slip through. The key is to listen first. Let them dig a hole for themselves. In one case I had planned to ask for fees of £10,000 per month, but I didn't answer the straight question of 'How much?' Eventually the client, after a preamble about how hard and competitive times were, asked us if we would mind working for a fee of just £20,000 a month at first until he could justify a budget increase to his boss. Surely the best return on investment for lunch at the Groucho an adman could hope for?'

£1-million-a-year adman

Here is a company chairman, the person, remember, that we agreed was charged with integrity, legality and the carrying out of standards and processes, asserting that sometimes it is right to forget the rules.

The performance angle

> *'A young person in any organization should know the limit of his or her authority, when to exceed it, and to make sure that he or she is right.'*
>
> A chairman

Question 61   *Is there a simple recipe for career success?*

No, but there are many that sound simple. Take this excellent piece of advice from the boardroom.

The people angle

> *'Choose a business that has an output you find enjoyable and interesting, always employ outstanding people beneath you, treat everyone with respect and accept that change is an opportunity not a threat.'*
>
> Chairman, FTSE 100 company

We have discussed above the difficulties of employing the right people; but it is the respecting everyone that gives most people problems. What happens when you are forced to work with someone whose abilities you suspect to be well below what is required, and/or whose work rate is less than needed? Continue to respect them by all means, but do not trust them to carry out the tasks allocated. Work round them and try to make them irrelevant to performance and deal with their manager until they get tired of it and address the performance issue. So, perhaps the chairman means us to respect everyone's right to a fair chance, but don't let it knock your results.

Question 62   *Do you wait for promotion or chase it?*

This one speaks for itself.

The performance angle

> *'If you know that you are performing well do not be afraid to ask for promotion or greater responsibility.'*
>
> George Paul, Chairman, Norwich Union

Question 63   *Are projects additional to your job opportunities or distractions?*

Managers do not get promoted if no one notices them. Extra tasks, like organising the staff party or helping with the monthly newsletter, raise your profile and get you noticed. In a world of quite a lot of froth and bubble, it is the out of the ordinary that brings managers into the inner circle. Chris Wathen broadens this concept to the whole world of possible business opportunities.

The people angle

'For those individuals who are motivated and aspire to the most senior leadership roles my advice would be to undertake many different, broad-ranging and stretching assignments. The key is to learn as much about the business environment as possible and develop an insight into the different disciplines that leaders need to understand to be successful. These include leading people, managing performance, marketing, operations, finance and technology. The world of business is becoming increasingly more challenging. Successful leaders will be those who retain clarity and focus in this demanding and ever more complex environment.'

Chris Wathen, Director of Human Resources, Natwest Group

Question 64   *It is difficult to understand your job in the context of the organization; so is it worth trying?*

It is absolutely essential if you want to get up amongst the strategic managers of the business. Start from linking your strategic plan to the ones above you (see question 23). What exactly do you mean by a strategy?

John Hart puts it beautifully.

The process angle

'At one time people were expected to simply get on with their job and not worry about the whole picture. These days people have to understand the whole of the business to ensure that they can work in a cross-matrix way and are able to move swiftly across the business to areas of greatest need.

In order to be successful it is important to have an understanding of what your organization wants, or needs from you, and how what you offer meets that need.'

John A Hart, Group Personnel Director, Powergen

Question 65   **With all these career politics and manoeuvrings is it essential actually to perform?**

Good point. Lest we forget:

The performance angle

> 'In building a career I have always thought it important that one should fulfil one's present job to the best of one' ability and, if one does well, promotion is likely to flow naturally although I appreciate that this is not always the case.
>
> 'Expressed in one line and accepting that it is something of a generality, my advice to people would be set your sights high but climb the stairs one at a time.'
>
> Sir David Lees, Chairman, GKN

Question 66   **Is it best to stay with one organization or move around?**

It has always been possible to have a number of jobs in your twenties, although some employers suspect and distrust 'job hoppers'. Nowadays circumstances change. A promise made to a member of staff in good faith may become impractical overnight. In this environment the safest view to take on your organization is that you owe it your loyal support only as long as your objectives and the organization's can co-exist. So, it is more a question of jobs now than careers. Companies do not offer jobs for life and most successful careerists will change employers from time to time. Keep an open mind and don't get so set in your ways that you get caught out by a reorganization in which you find yourself with the post 'co-ordinator of long-term planning'. Such a post almost certainly means that you are no longer part of those long-term plans.

The people angle

> '1 Aim high and achieve this by moving upwards between well-regarded organizations every two years.
> 2 Work on continual self-improvement, courses, private study, new qualifications, professional memberships, extra work projects, etc.
> 3 Be completely flexible on career moves that benefit. Relocate, move overseas, move to HQ and move again after a short period. Any career chance to progress up the ladder should be taken.'
>
> PR Williams, Group Human Resources Director, Vodafone AirTouch

There is an alternative to all this career manoeuvring business – settle for a quiet life at a level in the business that suits you. We cannot all be the chief executive, so set your sights to your own life/work objectives.

Section 8

MANAGING PROJECTS

Introduction

Project management provides structure, focus, flexibility, and control in the pursuit of results. This section describes what running a project entails and suggests ways to increase the likelihood of success.

By definition, a project is a series of activities designed to achieve a specific outcome within a set budget and timescale. It is important to distinguish projects from everyday work and adopt the discipline of project management more widely to improve performance.

So what is a project? A project has clear start and end points, a defined set of objectives, and a sequence of activities in between. The activities need not be complex: painting the staff restaurant is as valid a project as building a bridge. Many people are involved in projects without realising it – for example if they work in a special team, perhaps outside the normal business schedule, and to a deadline. Routine work on the other hand, is usually ongoing, repetitive and process-oriented. It is sometimes good to re-examine your everyday work to see if it lends itself to being managed as a project. If you tackle it as such you are likely to greatly increase your efficiency.

So why use formal project management? The competitive business environment means that a flexible and above all responsive approach to changing customer requirements is essential. Project management forces you to focus on priorities, performance, overcoming difficulties and adapting to change. All in all project management gives you more control if you use the proven tools and techniques to help you lead a team to reach objectives on time and within budget. It may seem that organising activities into project form is time consuming initially; but in the longterm it saves time, effort, and most importantly reduces the risk of failure.

Question 67 *How do you make sure all the appropriate people are involved?*

A senior manager in a large telephone operator told us recently that his most pressing problem was how to get each of several hundred project managers to pass information to each other and stop reinventing the wheel on a regular basis. There are also legions of projects where an outside interference arrives late in the day and negates a lot of time and effort previously spent. Identifying anyone who may have an interest or a contribution to make has to be the starting point of any project plan.

Involving the stakeholders

This is an interesting area of project management that frequently goes wrong. The only certainty about any complex project is that the jobs of some people are going to change. Most large organizations are getting better at managing such change. There are, however, still some, along with many smaller businesses, which handle this part of the process at best insufficiently and at worst with a lack of sensitivity. This imperils the implementation of the decision.

Incidentally, do not confuse this stage with training. It is helping the people involved to understand the benefits to their company, their customers and themselves of the change that the decision involves.

The people angle

Upsetting key people with technology

This is a good illustration of this point. It concerns the handling of a major electronic point of sale (EPOS) upgrade decision by a large supermarket chain. The chain in question had some 200 sites in the UK and wanted to introduce advanced EPOS, first in a pilot site and then throughout the group.

The objectives were set as follows:

- *to reduce time at checkout and improve customer satisfaction*
- *to improve stock control and shelf stocking activity*
- *to improve the productivity of checkout operators*
- *to improve job satisfaction both in the front of store and back of store areas.*

Given the volumes, margins and stock sensitivities of a supermarket, all the objectives were easy to build into a business case. Senior management recognized that the project would add many millions of pounds to the bottom line.

The IT people chose hardware and software and carried out training, albeit in the case of the pilot site just before the implementation. Engineers installed the equipment. It passed its acceptance tests and management looked forward to the results.

In fact the pilot was a disaster. Every single objective area produced a negative result. The queues were longer and shelf stocking actually got worse.

Customers' frustration took them to action that is the store manager's nightmare. They abandoned full trolleys near the checkouts. The process of replacing these items on the shelves is almost as expensive as throwing the whole lot away.

Staff were so upset that key and long-serving people were leaving or threatening to do so.

What had gone wrong? The resulting post mortem drew the conclusion that it was the early stage of the project that had misfired. The people in the stores were unaware of what was happening although fully aware that there was going to be some upheaval to their normal way of life.

The implementation managers found a simple solution for the roll out to other stores. During the build-up to each supermarket installing advanced EPOS, local management arranged a series of activities guided by a package of material developed centrally.

Thus store managers received a box of materials. Instructions helped them to put posters up at appropriate times signalling the approach of the new technology. Store managers distributed newspapers with information on advanced EPOS including crosswords and competitions to add some interest.

By the time training was due staff were comfortable with the concept and the implementation proceeded smoothly. In the event, the number of people involved with giving training courses diminished and the simple process paid for itself time and time again.

Identifying stakeholders

A stakeholder in a complex project is any individual or group of individuals who is affected in any way by it. They may be suppliers, people who will have to supply different products and services or even just go through a different buying process. They will certainly include customers. I mean, if your customers are not going to be affected by the project you are about to carry out, why are you doing it at all, and how have you stated the project purpose?

Stakeholders will include your boss as well as your team. Now think about other teams. Is your project going to be unsuccessful if other teams in the organization do not agree with it or buy into the implementation? If, for example, you are the manager of the help desk in the UK about to implement a different system for logging calls, would there be extra benefits to your customers, and therefore to the organization, if the system were adopted Europe-wide? If that is the case, it is much more sensible to get their buy-in before you start the project rather than trying to persuade them to go the same way after the event.

Now think about other people who could be working in the same area. Everyone becomes aware in the end of new methods and processes available to them to improve their performance. It is very unfortunate if managers keep important projects to themselves so that they can earn brownie points by being the first to make a change. How much better it is if they looked for the brownie points attracted by the manager who leads a group of peer groups towards some improvement in the way they do things.

Has anyone implemented a similar project in the fairly recent past? If so, then they should certainly be on your stakeholder list. Their input could be invaluable in helping you reach the best result.

So, how do you pull all this together and document it?

Table 8.1 Stakeholder analysis.

Stakeholder	I/E	Interest or involvement	I	+/–	S

The stakeholder column identifies the individuals or groups that will be most involved or impacted by this project. The next column (I/E) says whether they are internal or external to the organization of the project manager. It is worth noting that external stakeholders can be much more difficult to control, and therefore may need a higher level of monitoring. Now write down why the individual or group is involved in the project and what the impact will be on them or what their involvement will be.

The column marked I allows you to estimate, on a scale of one to five, the impact the stakeholder will have on the decision. If they could make or break it you will score it five. If their impact, for or against, is minimal then score it one. When you are running the project you will of course pay more attention to the stakeholders who score highly here. Now document their current attitude to the decision on a scale of five to minus five. Five means that the stakeholders are strongly supportive, zero that they are neutral and minus five that they believe that the project is ill-conceived and will try to stop its implementation. The status column is marked red, amber or green, depending on the amount of work that you are going to have to put in with this stakeholder. If there is little to do, mark it green, if the stakeholder could pose a big problem mark it red.

These numbers will change as you go through the project management process and communicate with the stakeholders to get their enthusiastic support.

Here is an example of a stakeholder analysis in the case of a fairly small project to change how salespeople tender for business in a technology company by writing more customer-oriented executive summaries.

Table 8.2   Stakeholder analysis for salespeople.

	Stakeholder	I/E	Interest or involvement	I	+/-	S
A	Marketing	I	Started the process off. Is looking for a template to write summaries faster.	4	0	A
B	Salespeople	I	Will have to be motivated to implement the decision.	5	-1	R
C	Tom Raseby	I	Salesman who could turn out to be a champion of the decision.	5	4	G
D	IT group	I	Will have to instal the software.	5	0	A
E	Financial controller Penny	I	Might have to OK the financial case.	3	0	A
F	Sales directors	I	Would be needed if the project is to go organization-wide.	3	0	A
G	European marketing manager	I	Could put a spanner in the works if they have a different idea.	2	0	G
H	Supplier	E	May have to modify the tool to meet the precise need. Must come up with a feasible cost.	4	5	G

Question 68   *How do you check the validity of every decision you make about a project?*

Using stakeholder analysis, you have just made a decision as to who should be on your list of stakeholders. Run it through the V-SAFE routine to test it out.

V for Value looks at the expected impact on the bottom line. Can we be sure that this decision will add value to the organization? The stakeholder list is without doubt valuable. All of these people could help you run a better project, and some of them could completely stop implementation if you do not at some point get their agreement and co-operation.

S for Suitable examines how this decision contributes towards strategy, and checks that it is appropriate given the current business situation. It is suitable by definition; they all belong on the list.

A is for Acceptable. Take a little time to think about how acceptable the stakeholders will find your project. You cannot be very specific on this, of course, since you have not even identified all the actions involved. But you will know, from the statement of purpose and list of issues, what problem you are setting out to solve. Will everyone you need agree that this is the right problem and that it should have some priority in terms of finding a solution? Already you will be sensitive to the people who will find it hard to accept. It is tempting to strike such potential 'blockers' off the list of stake-holders. After all, if you fail to persuade them to accept the need for the change, you may be unable to make decisions that address the real problem and have any chance of being implemented. And, of course, if you have the backing of your boss, maybe he or she can sort them out. Missing them out, however, would be a mistake. It is always better to beard the blockers in their den at the outset than leave them to become a hindrance during the project management process or, worse still, during the implementation.

F for Feasible checks that the decision is feasible given time and other constraints. In the case of the stakeholder list this might need some consideration. Are you going to be able to contact all of them in a way that makes sense to them and you? You might decide at this stage how you are going to consult them. Will you need to meet them face to face? Probably, at least with a representative of your customer. Will you have to involve others who are going to have their jobs changed with a presentation or demonstration of what the change will entail? Some of the others can be covered by an e-mail or a telephone call. This contact plan should tell you whether the list is achievable or not. Delete, with regret, those who are going to be affected but whom you will not have time to involve. It is better at this stage to make a decision not to see someone rather than leave them on the list knowing that you will never get round to it. You now know whether it is feasible for you to tackle the stakeholders on your list.

That just leaves **E for Enduring**. You need to check the validity of any project decision in terms of how long its suitability, etc. will last. You do not want to do something that has to be replaced in the short term. You can probably tell from your knowledge and experience whether or not the decision you are considering will stand the test of time, but there is a strategic element to this too. An enduring decision will have to fit in with the long-term strategy of the business.

The process angle

Having made good sales of computer equipment to one part of a large organization, a salesperson decided to mount a sales campaign on another operating company in the same group, using the initial customer as a compelling reference. He did not check that such a marketing decision would be enduring by comparing it with the published strategy of the corporation. This strategy involved moving the emphasis away from the second company's product markets.

After the salesperson had put in a lot of his time and resources, he was left high and dry when the corporation sold the target business out of the group.

Question 69   *How do you make sure you get a good start to a project?*

There is much more to the management of successful projects than simply developing a detailed plan. Project start-up must enable team leaders and project managers to create a project framework that significantly increases the probability of project success, and that the project's success is followed by real benefits to the organization.

Strong leadership and ownership are required and two roles are typically key to success. Firstly, the project sponsor, that is the initiator, the one who provides direction and the one who ensures resources are available as and when required. Secondly, the project manager who is responsible for fully developing the project plan and for monitoring and managing project activities. Whilst the same person sometimes performs these roles, there can also be advantages in keeping the roles separate.

There should be a sound rationale for initiating projects as they will detract from operations and consume limited resources.

The success of a project is directly related to the clarity of the vision or 'the desired changed state'. Before any project is confirmed, therefore, the benefits that are expected should be contrasted with the costs of completing the project in terms of resources consumed. This go/no-go decision will be repeated at every milestone to ensure that the project will ultimately add value.

Achievement of objectives should not just be checked at the end, but progress should be monitored and formally reviewed on completion of major project phases and on a regular time-driven basis. All change results in risks, but actions can typically be taken to minimize their effect, and this should be done proactively.

Visible commitment to change is often necessary to ensure ongoing availability of resources as and when required

Identify the main drivers of the project by listing the issues, the concerns, opportunities and threats that the project involves. Ask yourself what external trends or factors are driving this project. Think about why you are undertaking this particular project and why now – is there a window of opportunity? Add to the list the impact on business or team performance of each driver and how urgent it is. Make sure you know where there are links with other projects, past, present and future. That way you will discover if this project depends on other teams' activities and, very importantly, learn from the successes and failures of the past.

Now turn to the next key decision – what are the objectives of this project, and what will indicate whether the project has succeeded or failed at the end? Check these out with all the stakeholders. At this point they may well suggest you look at other activities going on in the organization so that you are not reinventing the wheel and that you are learning from others. What is the relative importance or priority of each indicator? Find the most important and give it a ten, then assess the remainder in relation to the most important one.

Finally, decide what the specific target to be achieved for each indicator is. You may, for example, have an objective to improve the company's performance in holding stock. One of the indicators will be to improve the stock to sales ratio – that is the indicator. The target may be to go from the current 30 days held in stock to 20. You can balance this indicator with another one that measures the number of times stock-outs dissatisfy customers. If the team understands the constraints it has to operate within, you can avoid the frustrations that occur when it comes up against some buffers in the implementation of the plan. What restrictions or constraints limit project activities? These are often set by the sponsor and typically include budgets or headcount limits. Knowing the reason for the constraint also helps the team's understanding.

Now identify the major phases of the project plan and put in place targets for what will be completed or delivered at the end of each phase. You may have to do the detailed project plan of activities before you are able to finalize these key milestones and the target date for completion. Work out the resources necessary to complete the project. How many person days will be consumed during each phase of the project? Include internal full-time and part-time people and the use of external contractors. Don't forget to work out what facilities will be required for each phase. Otherwise you may find yourself with requirements for equipment or physical space that will become a bottleneck; similarly with materials. From this you can calculate the target cost or budget for each phase and make sure that the purpose and objectives of the project outweigh the overall cost.

Expand the information you have about stakeholders and team members to cover, for example, the quickest and easiest way to communicate with each person or group.

Formal project start-up is essential to the smooth running of an implementation. It is more than the detailed project activity plan, if the project is to identify with and assist the overall objectives and strategy of the organization.

Question 70   *How do you take the project's risks into account?*

Every decision a manager takes carries risk. It is wise to use a consistent method of identifying risks and planning how to avoid the most serious ones or at least ameliorate the result if the risk actually occurs.

Here are the main principles of risk management that a consistent approach needs to pay attention to.

- All major projects or changes will carry some risks in terms of successful implementation and the achievement of the desired results.
- Teams should be proactive in identifying and prioritising risks.
- Where it is possible, decision-makers should take positive action to lower the likelihood that the risk will occur.
- Teams should plan reactive actions to minimize the effects of the risk if it occurs.

Notice the use of the word team in the principles statement. This is another area where people acting on their own are unlikely to do a thorough job. You need the power of a brainstorm to flush out all the possibilities. Who, then, should be in the risk assessment team?

People in the team will include those who will have a responsibility in implementing a decision or a plan, and those who, because perhaps of past experience, are in an advisory role. Look for people who have the information necessary to do the analysis, and those whose commitment is needed to take preventative actions or carry out contingency actions. You should expect this part of the decision-making process to be part logical thinking, the identification of risks, and part intuitive, the assessment of the chances of the risk occurring.

Make sure that the people involved are at the business end of the decision. That is, those people who will be hands-on in implementing the decision or the actions concerned with risk. It is interesting to note that small businesses or large businesses who emphasize the autonomy of their business units tend to avoid taking risks that would be very serious if the situation turns against them. We are discovering that, in the case of rail operators, it is much more likely for a company to avoid the catastrophe of a fatal accident if the people physically looking at the rails and testing them are responsible for the maintenance programme. It seems from experience that risk avoidance in those circumstances is much more likely if the board is taking decisions for the whole network based on the advice of a project manager with responsibility for the budget as well as performance.

The process angle

'To make the point I will exaggerate, but you know it would be hard to inflict lasting damage on Johnson & Johnson even if you wanted to because of our decentralization. In a highly centralized company, it is possible for either the CEO or a small group of executives to make one or a series of profound decisions that will affect the corporation for the next twenty years. It's terrific if they are right, and it's catastrophic if they are wrong.'

Ralph Larsen, Chairman, Johnson & Johnson
(as told to Spitzer and Evans (1997) Heads you Win, *Simon and Schuster*

Here is an example of the form that the team needs to fill in to identify and assess the risks of a decision.

	RISKS	P	I	ACTION TO MANAGE RISKS	S
A					
B					
C					
D					
E					
F					
G					
H					
I					
J					
K					
L					
M					
N					
O					

RISK ANALYSIS

Name	Phil Bracewell
Team	Sales/IT
Date	05-Apr-01
Status	Amber

TITLE: **Introduction of executive summary tool**

RISKS

Fig. 8.1 Risk management.

The first column is an identifier for references purposes. The second identifies the nature of the risk. Ask yourself what the potential problems associated with this activity are. What could go wrong? As a memory jogger or thought starter, the team might care to use these groupings:

- what could go wrong financially?
- what could go wrong technically?
- what could go wrong practically?

Since the last of these includes those aspects of performance that involve people changing how they do things, it is likely to be a large area of risk.

The third column marked 'P' is the team's intuitive feel for how likely it is that the risk will happen. Mark it ten if the chances of occurrence are more or less a certainty, and one where the risk is very unlikely to occur. Some risks have more impact on performance than others. Identify these by marking in the 'I' column the impact that the risk will have on performance or achievement of the decision's objectives. If the impact is low, a marginal impact only, then mark it one. If the impact is significant mark it up to ten.

Now look at what could be done to manage the risk. Look at this in two ways. What can you do to minimize the probability that the risk will occur, and how can you minimize the impact if it does occur? Finally assess the status of each risk, as red, immediate action is required, amber, future action is probably going to be required or green, where there is no action required either because the probability of its occurring is low or because the impact is low.

When should you perform risk analysis when making a decision? There are two important times really, whenever a change is about to be introduced, and whenever you are planning an activity that could have a significant impact on performance. This means that risk assessment is not confined to the time when you are actually taking a decision, but will occur subsequently as you implement the plan that flowed from the decision.

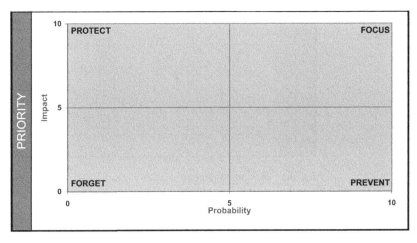

Fig. 8.2   Risk analysis.

Figure 8.2 shows a diagram of the impact and urgency. Those risks with low impact and low probability of occurrence we can more or less forget, while those in the high probability, but low impact, quarter we would look at in terms of assessing whether or not it is worthwhile trying to prevent the occurrence. In the top left corner, where the impact is high but the probability low, we should look for ways to protect ourselves against occurrence and mitigate the impact if they do occur. But the overwhelming focus for action is those risks that lie in the top right hand quarter where the probability is high and so is the impact.

The people angle

Frequently the highest impact and urgency quarter will refer to the problem of people resisting the changes that the project brings with it. Miss out a significant number of these people, and the whole project is at risk. You need 20% of the people involved to welcome the change if it is to be made successfully, so make sure that you have at least that number of people backing the action.

Section 9

MANAGING CHANGE

Question 71   *How do you make sure that your products and services are competitive in a changing world?*

In today's competitive environment, teams and companies must deliver what the customer needs and at a level of performance that has some advantage over the competition. Customer value analysis enables the team or company's performance to be assessed against customer selection or purchase criteria, and against the competition. In many ways it looks at a product/market in the same way as a salesperson looks at a particular customer during a complex sales campaign.

The primary purpose of customer value analysis is to understand the factors driving customer value and competitive positioning and by so doing make a plan to maximize value. It starts from understanding the basis on which customers make decisions and what the main drivers are of their businesses in the case of corporates, or the main benefits they are seeking in the case of consumers. The basis of competition will vary across customer groups and across product groups.

In-depth analysis of customers and competitors takes time and effort; so give priority to customer and product groups of greatest potential value. Similarly from the customers' point of view there will be many factors that influence choice, but they will not all be of equal importance or influence.

Wherever there are competitors, there is customer choice. Success also, therefore, requires an understanding of competitor performance. Winning business requires a unique selling proposition that clearly answers the question: 'Why will this customer buy this product or service from us as opposed to our competition?'

Try, in the first place, to identify and classify the customer's basis of decision. Ask yourself what criteria they use to decide to buy. If this is difficult or you find yourself guessing, you need to do some market research to come up with the list. In this regard market research may be no more than speaking to some customers who have recently bought from you or a competitor and asking them what was important to them as they made their decision.

Now classify the criteria by the area that each criterion primarily relates to:

- product – features or attributes of the product or service itself
- process – aspects of the way the product or service is delivered
- people – the way in which the relationship is managed
- price – aspects of cost, purchase price of value.

For each criterion:

1   Find out what the customer's ideal solution is.
2   Estimate the relative importance to the customer of each criterion by giving the most important one ten and then rating the remainder in relation to the most important one.
3   Work out how your product or service offering performs against the ideal. Score ten if there is a perfect fit, and zero if the fit is poor.
4   Work out how the product or service offering of your direct competitor performs against the ideal. Score ten if there is a perfect fit, and zero if the fit is poor.
5   Finally, decide the status of your performance against each criterion:
   - red – immediate action is required (your competitor performs better than you against the most important criteria)
   - amber – future action is probably going to be required
   - green – no action is required.

This final action makes sure that you do something to improve your competitiveness in those areas where you know the customer has real concerns that may take them to the competition.

Carry out customer value analysis on a regular basis to monitor trends and whenever you are entering a new market or launching a new product or service. You also need to do it whenever a new potential customer or new competitor enters the market.

Question 72   *How do you get enough impetus behind a major change?*

Managing change can be a depressing business but there is hope in one simple rule. There has been research in production and other environments to support a rule of thumb that we have found to be true practically. If you have to manage a change process you need 'agents of change' to support you. Agents of change are people who fundamentally agree with the need for change and have the will to go through the process themselves.

The people angle

A European electricity supply company that was preparing to become a private company having belonged to the state all its life needed to write strategic plans for all its power stations.

Senior management knew that there would be fierce resistance to the changes that had to be made, and they decided to include the whole management team of each power station in planning the new strategy. This produced rather large planning teams of up to twenty people, but seemed the right way to go. The resistance differed from station to station and a pattern emerged. In the more progressive stations where, say, 50% of the team could be regarded as agents of change either before the planning session or after it, senior management could already see the first signs of successful change. If, at the planning session, there were 20%, it was harder work but it could be made to happen. Below that it looked and turned out to be hopeless. And of course there was one where no agent of change appeared, not even the station manager, and they failed there. So the rule of 20% is a practical one.

Question 73   *Why are business processes so important in managing change?*

We will leave two pioneers in the field to explain this.

Charles Kepner and Benjamin Tregoe found that people were unwilling to get into discussion on important changes if there was no systematic procedure to follow. They argued that it was difficult for people to discuss decisions about change because the participants in the discussion often felt that important aspects would be missed out, or that there would be options, outside the ones being promoted by members of the team, that would be missed by the group. This leads to what Kepner and Tregoe called making decisions about change through the 'shoving process', in which the person with the most power is bound to prevail.

But if people are given a common approach to project management, the teamwork improves and the decisions arrived at depend on the activities and thinking processes of the whole team. That is, it is the systematic process that stops project management being a one-person activity and allows brainstorming techniques to offer more creative options and reach a better decision.

They said:

'Decision analysis, for example, is a systematic procedure based on the thinking pattern we use when making choices. Its techniques represent expansion and refinement of the elements in this thinking pattern:

we appreciate the fact that a choice must be made;

we consider the specific factors that must be satisfied if the choice is
to succeed;
we decide what kind of action will best satisfy these factors; and
we consider what risks may be attached to our final choice of action
that could jeopardize its safety and success.'

Kepner and Tregoe (1997) The New Rational Manager, *Princeton*
Research Press.

Question 74   *How do I get someone to accept a change when I know they won't like it when it happens?*

Get them involved in trying it out. There is a sales technique called a puppy
dog close that can often be adapted to help someone to welcome change.

The close is based on the activities of a person who sell pets. 'Look,' he says
to Mum and Dad, 'why don't you take the puppy home for the weekend and
see how the kids get on with it. No obligation, if you don't want it I'll come
round on Monday and take it away.' What with? A small army?

The salesperson knows that by the end of the weekend the kids will be as
willing to give up the little dog as they are to give up breathing or having a
birthday. This technique is used by many industries in various ways, and is
linked to the idea of making sales by inertia. When did you last get an offer
to send in a direct debit for a magazine subscription with the promise that
no debits would be made until you had received your four free issues? That's
a puppy dog close.

They are using it for credit cards nowadays and even IT equipment and
software. It works where the product, once experimented with, becomes
highly desirable or where the customer continues with the product because
they don't know how to stop it coming, or they can't be bothered. Book clubs
would hardly exist without this close.

Ken has just received the *Wall Street Journal* free for four weeks. In the
end he declined to pay for it in future and sent the direct debit confirmation
back marked cancelled. They sent him another one to make sure, with the
extraordinary PS: 'This is a **risk-free** offer. If you choose not to continue, the
four weeks are yours to keep free of charge.' You mean there was a risk they
might have asked for their old newspapers back?

Translate this into the change process and see if it works.

Question 75   *What steps do I have to take people through to get their agreement to change?*

Look at the person whose behaviour you want to change. To begin with they
may very well be in **denial** – they do not recognize what the change is or why
they need to accept it. As you explain to them the reasons for the change
make sure you cover all the angles. What is in it for the customer, the organization and, above all, the person you are addressing? At worst, the person

will move from denial to **resistance**. They will find a hundred reasons why the status quo is preferable.

You have to move them carefully into **exploration**. Make them familiar with how things will be when the change has happened and slowly remove their fears. Be sincere in your wish to consult with them, and be prepared to accept their suggestions if they are not at odds with the objective of the change project.

Finally, look for **commitment**. Make sure that there is some reward for their wholehearted acceptance of the change. Eventually they will **internalize** the change and accept the new situation as the norm.

Section 10

STARTING YOUR OWN BUSINESS

Introduction

We have been independent consultants for a number of years. We therefore hear frequently asked questions on the topic of leaving a large company and setting up on your own. Here are some of those questions and our best responses drawn from experience. Some questions are on consultancy, the rest applicable to any small business.

Question 76   *How do I define my overall aim in setting up my own business?*

The best advice you can get from successful people who have done it is the source of much of this section. All of them are agreed on one thing – don't mix up your objectives. Take, for example, advice on the type of person to hire into your business; it is quite different depending on your objective. If you are trying to build the 'best' or the 'biggest' you will have to hire really good people and take on board the problems such people inevitably bring with them. If your concern is to live the way you want unfettered by outsiders' demands, you no more want the hassles of the creative and bright than you want a heron on your goldfish pond.

Eventually the options boil down to three.

- **Money**
  Some people simply want to be rich. They want to make a lot of money as quickly as possible and then retire early to spend more time with their grown-up families than they ever did when their children were young. To do this they have to build a business with apparent shareholder value that they can sell in, probably, an earn-out allowing them to do another three years in the business before retiring as one of the richest five hundred in the land. The decisions that such people take will be as consistent as possible with the well-being of the business as such, but the overriding objective is their personal wealth and they will take risks with the business in that regard. As one of them so neatly put it, 'OK, maybe we are growing a bit too fast for the theorists, but I don't want to have to dig my own swimming pool.' Often charming, sometimes simply frightening,

these people know exactly what they want and will work hard and do whatever is necessary to make that happen. Don't, incidentally, get in their way if you are a 'quiet life' person. Their strengths include their enthusiasm and their ability to understand instantly the way they should take their business forward – the aiming point is easy to identify. The successful ones discover new insights in how to manage a business for owner's profit, and everyone can learn from them.

- **Fame**
  Other people want to build a business to make a name for themselves. They will happily appear in their own advertisements and punt themselves as gurus to the broadcasters and press at any opportunity. They desire a high profile, an OBE at least, and eventually seats on government agencies that pay very little or nothing but give them cocktail party access to the great and the good. They too will work hard and do what is necessary to fulfil their dream. Their strengths include their unquenchable self-belief and single-mindedness. Add to that the amount of free publicity they can generate to advance their businesses and you can see the connection between their ambition and their companies' success. If they have a weakness it can be suspicion and fear of other talented people in the business whom they think might eclipse their reputation as being, in fact '*the* person in the one-person business'. I knew one who declared that he wanted inscribed on the tombstone above his grave the epitaph 'He was the founder of Esprit,' Esprit being the name of his company. I forbore from telling him that his attitude to his senior people whom he had messed up on the way was likely to make them search that grave out so that they could dance on it.

- **Lifestyle**
  Some people tire of the rat race and want to get out to build a more suitable lifestyle. As we have said, that ambition will influence dramatically how they run their businesses. Their personal lives are completely mixed in with their business lives, and decision-making on the latter will always start from the former. Often they are fulfilling their life-long passion or hobby and turning it into a business that will probably not put them up with the mega rich, and certainly not make them feature in the national press, but that is not their dream, and that is not how they define success.

So, which are you? All three objectives obey the attributes of a good objective. They are:
- measurable – you will know when you have achieved the dream
- achievable – many people have succeeded before you and often not the most likely people, so by following common sense rules you can build the business of your dreams
- time targeted – you have to know when you want to get there, because we are a long time dead.

But most of all they are specific and clear. They give the aiming point and thus define the opening, middle and end games. So take a moment to decide what you want to do, and then read on to discover from a combination of people's experiences and sound business practices how to get there.

Question 77 *How do I assess if I would be capable of and enjoy starting my own business?*

'Know yourself' was the motto above the oracle at Delphi and gives good advice. From the attributes people have discussed with us as important we have put together this simple self-assessment scheme to give a clear indication of whether or not you are a suitable case for joining the ranks of the small business person or entrepreneur. How well do the following attributes describe you? Answer the following statements with:

1 = yes
2 = mainly
3 = not really
4 = no.

Table 10.1 Self assessment.

Statement	Score			
I am a good listener	1	2	3	4
I hate putting things off	1	2	3	4
I tackle hard jobs before easy ones	1	2	3	4
The family supports my decision to set up on my own	1	2	3	4
I am ready to work all day, every day when necessary	1	2	3	4
I have good self-discipline	1	2	3	4
I can sell	1	2	3	4
I like selling	1	2	3	4
I take decisions carefully	1	2	3	4
I deal well with stress	1	2	3	4
I learn from my mistakes	1	2	3	4
I take advice	1	2	3	4
I can motivate people	1	2	3	4
I can think long-term	1	2	3	4
I enjoy working on my own	1	2	3	4
I hate office politics getting in the way of company objectives	1	2	3	4
I can do without the trappings of big companies – for example, kick off meetings, award ceremonies, company sponsorship and parties	1	2	3	4
I like to be in control	1	2	3	4
I prefer to work to objectives rather than carry out tasks	1	2	3	4
I understand the risks of going on my own	1	2	3	4

Analysis

Add up your score by totalling the numbers in the boxes you have marked.

Score 70–80. You are not, by your own estimation, the type to go plunging into a small entrepreneurial business. Use this book as a guide to building your empire within a large organization.

Score 50–70. Hmm. You have some of the traits of a plunger but have another look at the areas where you scored 3 or 4 and ask yourself if you could, with practice, improve. If the answer to that is yes, then have a go by all means but be prepared for a few sleepless nights.

Score 30–50. Go on, go for it. You don't enjoy the big company that much and think of the benefits.

Score 20–30. What are you waiting for, stupid, you are a natural. You should have done it years ago so come on in, the water's terrifying.

Hang on, you have only done the easy part of 'Know thyself'. Now ask your nearest and dearest and then some trustworthy colleagues to agree or disagree with your own assessment.

Question 78   *Is becoming an independent consultant as lucrative as it seems?*

Becoming a consultant is a lifestyle objective in the main, although if you get it right the money can be good as well. Good but limited, because there are only so many days that you can sell. You will not become famous or build the biggest company in the business unless you take on one of the most difficult management tasks of them all – managing other consultants. Many people do it in their middle thirties and another load do it later when they take early retirement from large organizations. Be prepared for a rather lonely working life. Around Christmas time your clients will all at some time say, 'Right, I have got to go now: we have one of our Christmas parties on today.' And you just go off, briefcase in hand, back to the office or spare room where you have set up the headquarters of your consultancy.

Be prepared also for a fair amount of stress. If you are in training, for example, you may well run the same type of course or even exactly the same course for many years. You will find this becomes stressful because by the time you have run it, say, thirty times you will be so familiar with the material that you will find it hard to believe that anyone does not know this stuff already. You also have the stress of selling enough days to make a living, not just the first year when all is exciting and fresh, but also every single year. No one else is accountable for getting you business.

Finally there is a stress in always being the person in charge. You go to the planning meeting, 'OK how do we start?' You go to the seminar and it is up to you to lead the move from the coffee room to the classroom and your job to start the whole thing off. Then there are your sales calls that are also up to you. But the benefits are also excellent. You report to nobody. (In fact after quite a short time you probably become unemployable.) And you organize your own life. It does not matter when you work. Some people prefer to work Saturday mornings, for example, when the telephone does not ring.

When you become a consultant it is easy to be misled into thinking that the money is really rather good. It is paid gross of tax, and if you work things correctly you may not have to pay any income tax for up to eighteen months. This inflates your income significantly. No one, of course, has deducted your contribution to a pension plan, and it may take a while for you to set one up. Then there are the expenses of being in business on your own. Think of these items. They are only the cash items; there will be depreciation on fixed assets as well:

- rent and rates
- buildings insurance
- business and liability insurance
- light and heat, even if you are working at home
- cleaning
- repairs and maintenance
- printing, postage and stationery
- telephone
- motor running expenses
- bookkeeping fees
- accountant's fees
- bank charges and interest
- books and research
- marketing and advertising.

These expenses could easily add up to not far short of twenty thousand pounds. If you are replacing a gross salary of £30,000, therefore, you need turnover of:

expenses	£20,000
salary	£30,000
pension	£4500
total	£54,500

Now consider the number of days you have available to earn that money. After deduction of weekends, holidays and bank holidays there are about 240 days left in the year.

From experience it is very hard to work more than 140 days actually on site as a consultant. This is different from a contractor who can work more or less all 240 days because they are more like employees than consultants. Consultants have marketing to do, sales calls to make, demonstrations to prepare and preparation work to do for most of the days they work and earn fees.

Here then are the required daily rates to support five different salary levels given sales of 140 or 100 days. Make sure you can charge at least these amounts, or you may find yourself worse off as a consultant than as an employee.

Table 10.2   Daily rates.

Gross salary to be replaced	**£30,000**	**£40,000**	**£50,000**	**£75,000**	**£100,000**
Pension	£4,500	£6,000	£7,500	£11,250	£15,000
Expenses	£20,000	£20,000	£20,000	£20,000	£20,000
Total	£54,500	£66,000	£77,500	£106,250	£135,000
Daily rate for 140 days	£389	£471	£554	£759	£964
Daily rate for 100 days	£545	£660	£775	£1063	£1350

Question 79   *I have a great product, should I set up a business to sell it?*

There is no such thing as a product without a market, just as there is no such thing as a market if you do not have a product for it. So, think in terms of 'product markets'.

When you have been on your own for a while and particularly if you meet a lot of middle managers in your clients' premises, you will be surprised how many people are thinking of doing the same as you, leaving the big company and going out on their own. They will speak to you about their ideas and ask for your comments. Usually they take what is probably the wrong approach. They have, for example, thought of, or developed and used, a management process or method of training that they believe could become their product. They have computerized it and think that with a bit of investment and work, that it could become marketable. And they could be right.

Unfortunately this gives them a product but not a product market. They do not have a product market until they have a customer. So this becomes good advice. Don't worry about products. There is a network of independent consultants out there who have a process or a training course, or a piece of software or whatever, to do anything a company might want to do, and, frankly, thousands of things companies will never want to do. And they will happily license you to sell it and deliver it or will equally happily pay you 15% of the gross fees if you pass them a customer.

In other words concentrate, when you are thinking of going into consultancy, on having a customer to work for immediately you are out, and the product side will look after itself. Assume you can do anything with a bit of help from your colleagues and work on the relationships with people in your current company or in your customers' or suppliers' companies so that when the great day dawns you can work out what they need and find, through the network, a method of satisfying that need.

It is quite easy to tag yourself into an appropriate network. Find out who are in similar skill areas to the ones you are going to bring to market and talk to as many of them as possible. But for your selling work, concentrate first on bringing a market to a product market, because that is the right way round.

Question 80   *Should I discount to get business?*

A sales manager quickly learns that success breeds success. If you have a salesperson well on target early on in the company year, you find that their selling and order taking actually improves. They are exuding confidence and maybe saying to customers some things that they may have held back from if they were desperate for sales. It is a kind of controlled arrogance. 'Look do you want the product or not?'

The opposite shows itself when a salesperson is up against it. They are only on twenty per cent of target with only two months to go. They put pressure on their prospects; they surprise their customers with heavy-handed tactics and so on. Customers can smell fear and they don't like it.

So it is with consultancy. If you are sure that there is a market for your services (and you did the research didn't you?), keep your confidence up and act happy. Play hard to get and do not be too available. Once you show anxiety and start to cut your daily rate, you are in trouble. Courage, work hard, work smart but don't give off even a subtle tinge of fear.

Question 81   *How flexible does an independent have to be?*

Very. The managing director of a chain of theme pubs says: 'A single creative act generates a stream of other creative acts.' Don't get too staid and fixed in the offerings you take to market. You will be surprised, when you have got going a bit, to find yourself going into situations that you did not envisage in your plan. As long as you know that you can offer a first class service, take on some different things. Sometimes the flow can take you into new sources of revenues and new product markets.

Question 82   *I have been offered seed money as a loan against my house, should I take it?*

The easiest way to borrow money for a new business is to agree that the owner's house should be mortgaged against the loan. You should resist this at all costs. If your business does not make it, it will be a nasty time to be homeless. If it all goes wrong at least you could sell or let your house until you got yourself fixed up with another source of income. It can be done. Use your track record as a businessperson to persuade lenders that you are likely to make the business a success. Make the plan look achievable and not pie in the sky. Speak to more than one potential lender, play one off against another and negotiate a different kind of guarantee.

Be careful, as banks will sometimes only ask for a personal guarantee rather than a mortgage on your house. If you own the whole of your house it has the same effect.

Section 11

THREE USEFUL PROCESSES

Introduction

Much of a manager's job depends on gathering useful information in time to assist with a decision. Sometimes we underestimate how business processes can help us in gathering that information and evaluating it. This is true even when the knowledge you are dealing with is highly subjective. The topic of understanding the financial health of an organization has never been more in doubt since, for example, the Enron affair. But the basics still work and the starting point for examining financial health remains the same – a process for interpreting an annual report in order, for example, to learn more about your own company, a supplier or a customer. The second process is a simple one for ranking business ideas. This makes decision-making better informed as you decide on which of several options is the best way ahead. This also uses the V-SAFE process of testing the merit of any option that you are deciding on.

The third process addresses the problem that all organizations struggle with – how do you spread knowledge and experience around the organization to prevent duplication of effort? Companies have tried many ways of doing this, suggestion boxes, incentive schemes for recording insights and so on. Our approach is to implement a simple business solution process that captures experience. In all cases the use of the electronic version of the tool, available from SofTools, can greatly increase the usefulness of the processes.

Question 83 How do you work out the key financial ratios from a company's annual report?

There are a number of ways that people do this, but we have found the following simple model gives you a clear picture of a company's financial health.

- Using this model gives a consistent measure and makes sure that you are comparing apples with apples.
- The directors' statements give a well-presented advertisement for the company. The figures tell the underlying story.
- Frequent use of this tool keeps the financial side of managing a business in the forefront of the mind.

Table 11.1 shows the figures you need to input to the model.

Table 11.1   Figures to be input to ratio model. (*Continued.*)

Ref	Term	Explanation	Notes
A	Sales	Sales outside the group excluding VAT	Also known as: Net sales Sales turnover Sales revenue
B	Net profit before tax	This is the profit before charging tax or extraordinary items	Almost always uses these words on the profit and loss account
C	Interest payable	Gross interest payable	Often on the balance sheet it shows net interest. The notes will give the gross figure payable
D	Depreciation	A method by which the full cost of an asset is charged against profit over the useful life of the asset.	Can often be found on the cashflow statement or notes to it
E	Tangible fixed assets	Those assets, like property, machinery, etc., that a company uses to generate income over a long period	Use the amount shown on the face of the balance sheet
F	Intangible fixed assets	Fixed assets without physical substance, such as licences, goodwill and patents	Many balance sheets do not include any intangible assets
G	Other fixed assets	Assets that are neither of the above	Predominantly these are: Investments Trade investments
H	Stocks	Trading and other stocks including raw materials, work in progress and finished goods	Also known as: Inventory
I	Trade debtors	Amounts receivable from customers. The balance sheet often has debtors and you have to go to the note to separate out trade debtors	Also known as: Accounts receivable
J	Total current assets	The sum of all those assets that would normally be turned into cash within one year	
K	Trade creditors	Amounts owed to suppliers. The balance sheet often has creditors and you have to go to the note to separate out trade creditors	Also known as: Accounts payable
L	Short-term loans	Loans payable within one year. This will include overdrafts and obligations under leases	There is often only one line to indicate all the short-term liabilities: Creditors: amounts due within one year. So you may have to go to the notes to find the short-term loans within this heading
M	Total current liabilities	The sum of all those liabilities that have to be paid within one year	Also known as: Creditors: amounts due within one year
N	Long-term loans	Loans repayable after more than one year	
O	Provisions for liabilities and charges	Includes deferred tax and other provisions	

Table 11.1   (*Continued.*)

Ref	Term	Explanation	Notes
P	Other long-term liabilities	Any other long-term liability not yet transferred to the tool	If you have had to go to the notes for the breakdown of long-term liabilities, make sure you have transferred any liabilities not covered by the previous two items
Q	Total shareholders' funds	The total of funds belonging to the shareholders including undistributed profits known as reserves	Use the figure described as the total
R	Minority interests	The amount of reserves that belongs to shareholders in non-wholly-owned subsidiaries	Quite often there are no minority interests
S	Average number of employees	Make sure you express this figure in the same units as the other figures	If, for example, the units used are £m, then 55,367 employees would be input as .055367
T	Employees' remuneration	Use the wages and salaries figure. Do not include social security or pension costs	There is no requirement to give this number in the USA, so many companies do not

Using the information in Table 11.1 the following figures can be calculated by the model.

Table 11.2   Figures calculated by the model. (*Continued.*)

Ref	Term	Explanation	Notes
AA	Total fixed assets $=E+F$	Tangible fixed assets plus intangible fixed assets	
BB	Total assets $=E+F+G+J$	The sum of the book value of all assets owned by the company	
CC	Total liabilities $=M+N+O+P+R$	Total current liabilities plus long-term loans and other long-term liabilities including provisions and minority interests	
DD	Net assets $=BB-M$	Total assets less current liabilities	This figure is often given on the balance sheet, so you can use it to check your input
EE	Capital employed $=N+O+P+Q+R$	Represents capital employed in the company from shareholders and other long-term sources	Check that net assets (DD) equals this number. If it does not, you have made a mistake at the input stage
FF	Quick assets $=J-H$	Total current assets minus stock, gives those current assets that can definitely be turned into cash quickly	
GG	Total debt $=L+N$	Total loans outstanding – short-term plus long-term	

Table 11.2   *(Continued.)*

Ref	Term	Explanation	Notes
HH	Net worth =Q–F	Shareholders funds less intangible assets	Intangible assets may be suspect, so some ratios will be calculated from net worth
II	Pre-interest profit =B+C	Profit available to meet the demands of shareholders and the providers of loans. Often described as EBIT – Earnings before interest and tax	Earnings and profits have the same meaning in this context
JJ	Net working capital =J–M	Total current assets less total current liabilities	This is money tied up in the business, and shareholders want it to go round the working capital cycle as fast as possible

Key business ratios – profitability

Table 11.3 shows the formulae for working out profitability.

Table 11.3   Profitability ratios.

Ref	Term	Explanation	
P1	Return on capital employed =B/EE	Pre-tax profit expressed as a percentage of capital employed	One of the most important ratios, showing how well the directors are using the shareholders' funds
P2	Profit margin B/A	Pre-tax profit expressed as a percentage of sales	
P3	Return on assets =B/BB	Pre-tax profits expressed as a percentage of total assets	
P4	Shareholders return =B/HH	Pre-tax profit expressed as a percentage of tangible net worth	

Key business ratios – liquidity

Table 11.4 shows the formulae for working out liquidity.

Table 11.4   Liquidity.

Ref	Term	Explanation	Notes
L1	Current ratio = J/M	The ratio of current assets to current liabilities	
L2	Quick ratio = FF/M	The ratio of current assets less stock to current liabilities	Also known as the acid test

Key business ratios – asset utility
> Table 11.5 shows the formulae for working out asset utility.

Table 11.5   Asset utility.

Ref	Term	Explanation	
A1	Stock turnover =A/H	The number of times stock is turned over during a year	Sometimes calculated as the number of days stock is held on average
A2	Collection period 365*I/A	The average amount of time expressed in days that customers take to pay invoices	
A3	Asset turnover =A/BB	Sales as a percentage of total assets	Sometimes called asset utilization

Key business ratios – gearing
> Table 11.6 shows the formulae for working out gearing.

Table 11.6   Gearing.

Ref	Term	Explanation	Notes
G1	Capital gearing =N/Q+N	A comparison of debt with shareholders' funds	
G2	Income gearing =C/II	Interest as a percentage of pre-interest profit	How much of the company's profits does it take to pay the interest bill? Many see this as the key gearing ratio

Key business ratios – employee
> Table 11.7 shows the formulae for working out employee ratios.

Table 11.7   Employee ratios.

Ref	Term	Explanation	Notes
E1	Sales per employee =A/S	Sales divided by employees	Shows how productive the employees are in generating sales
E2	Profit per employee = B/S	Pre-tax profits divided by employees	Shows how productive the employees are in generating profits
E3	Average wage per employee =T/S	Employee remuneration divided by the number of employees	Checks how competitive the company is in paying staff

Key business ratios – growth ratios

Table 11.8 shows the formulae for working out growth ratios.

Table 11.8   Growth ratios.

Ref	Term	Explanation	Notes
S1	Sales growth	This calculation subtracts the previous year figure from the current year and expresses the result as a percentage of the previous year	
S2	Profit growth	This calculation subtracts the previous year figure from the current year and expresses the result as a percentage of the previous year	

Question 84   How do I decide on the relative values of one business idea compared to another?

New ideas schemes often fail because they generate too few or too many ideas that don't get implemented. Here is a mechanism for the generation and capture of new ideas, and then the systematic evaluation of each idea against five generic criteria. It aims to generate and exploit new feature, product, market or business ideas.

It is no longer good enough to sustain yesterday's performance – as customer expectations rise and competitors improve, our performance must also continuously improve. Structured and systematic approaches to brainstorming can significantly improve the quality and quantity of new ideas generated. Whilst some people are naturally more creative than others, everyone can improve their ability to generate new ideas simply through the adoption of tools and techniques.

Not all new ideas are good ideas so once the ideas have been generated they must be prioritized, and only the best new ideas developed. Innovation sessions should be run whenever there is a need to challenge the status quo or current way of doing things – this may be triggered by falling market share or simply complaints from dissatisfied customers.

In any event it is useful to conduct regular creativity sessions involving a cross-functional team – perhaps on a quarterly basis.

The ideas portfolio process

Give a name to all of the ideas of new features, products, markets or businesses using brainstorming or other creative techniques.

Now describe the idea in terms of its purpose and key features. Think particularly about the impact of the idea on your customer. Note who was responsible for generating the idea, whether an individual or a team. Then go through the V-SAFE quick evaluation process.

What is the relative value – 'V' – of each idea? Ten indicates dramatic

TITLE		IDEA DESCRIPTION	INITIALS	V	S	A	F	E	%	R
1									0%	
2									0%	
3									0%	
4									0%	
5									0%	
6									0%	
7									0%	
8									0%	
9									0%	
10									0%	
11									0%	
12									0%	
13									0%	
14									0%	
15									0%	
16									0%	
17									0%	
18									0%	
19									0%	
20									0%	
21									0%	
22									0%	
23									0%	

IDEAS PORTFOLIO

Name
Team
Date
Status

TITLE

Fig. 11.1   Ideas portfolio.

impact on strategy and the overall business while one indicates a marginal impact on operating performance.

How suitable – 'S' – is each idea? A score of ten fits perfectly with current activities, products and markets while a score of one indicates that it would require significant change to the way operations are managed.

How acceptable – 'A' – would each idea be to all those impacted by it? A score of ten indicates the idea is positively supported by all stakeholders while a score of one indicates that it is resisted by most stakeholders.

How feasible – 'F' – is each idea given current time and resource constraints? A score of ten indicates that it fits within current budgets while a score of one means the idea would be extremely difficult to get funding for.

Will the idea endure – 'E' – over the short and long term? A score of ten indicates that it is totally consistent with and supports the long-term strategic development. A score of one indicates short-term impact only with a very limited window of opportunity.

How does each idea perform as a percentage of the ideal? Calculate this from the answers to the above. Finally note the team's recommendation for each idea. G = Go; W = Wait; N = No-Go; R= Research.

Question 85   *How do I record the solution to a business problem for future use?*

On a daily basis around most large organizations, the same problems are being fixed by different people in different ways – resulting in duplication of effort and wasted time and money. This third process enables individuals and teams to capture effective solutions to known business problems in a format that enables others to reapply them time and time again. Its purpose is to ensure the effectiveness of continuous improvement initiatives and maximize the re-use of solutions to business problems (avoiding reinventing the wheel).

Solutions to business problems should be captured so that others in the future can benefit from the lessons learnt by one person. A systematic approach will help to ensure that all aspects of the problem have been thought through and that the fix will not simply be short-term. It is often necessary to understand the cause of a problem before a solution can be determined and put in place. A culture of continuous business innovation or improvement is required to compete effectively in today's competitive environment.

Try to go through the process whenever a fix has been put in place for a business problem that may recur in other teams or in the future. The tool can also be used to provide a quick structured methodology for problem solving.

First of all, record the facts relating to the business problem. It may be necessary to conduct analysis or to validate facts before jumping to a solution.

			BUSINESS SOLUTIONS	Name / Team / Date / Status

TITLE

		TOPIC	FACTS RELATING TO THE BUSINESS PROBLEM
UNDERSTAND	U1	Business area impacted	
	U2	Problem description	
	U3	Impact on performance	
	U4	Problem timing	
	U5	Problem location	
	U6	Groups impacted	

		TOPIC	SOLUTION TO ADDRESS THE PROBLEM
DECIDE	D1	Root cause	
	D2	Solutions considered	
	D3	Solution selected	
	D4	Reason for selection	
	D5	Solution KSFs	

		TOPIC	ACTIONS TAKEN TO IMPLEMENT THE SOLUTION
ACT	A1	Phase 1	
	A2	Phase 2	
	A3	Phase 3	
	A4	Phase 4	
	A5	Phase 5	

		TOPIC	OUTCOME AND LEARNING FOR THE FUTURE
LEARN	L1	Outcome & results	
	L2	Future implications	
	L3	Potential problem 1	
	L4	Potential problem 2	
	L5	Potential problem 3	

Fig. 11.2   Business solutions.

What solution was chosen and what were the reasons? Make sure the solution dealt with the underlying problem, not just the effect of it.

The performance angle

Your washing machine is leaking. Finding cause is not a complex process; you follow the water trail from where you saw it back to its source. It's a hose. It has frayed a bit and obviously leaks water, not all the time because when you got to it the machine was empty and the leak more or less dried up. You decide that the leak is very small and stick a bowl under the hose to catch the drips, vowing to check it from time to time and empty it if it is nearly full. Your decision is aimed at the effect. It has solved the problem with the least amount of effort and time. It could be that you will forget to empty the bowl and the floor will get wet again, and it could be that the leak if unfixed will get worse until eventually the hose bursts dramatically and you have a major flood. But that is for the long term.

Typically, managers are working on the effects of problems. That gives you the quickest results although frequently not the cheapest. Managers who are working almost solely on effects are said to be fire-fighting and are unlikely to be changing their organizations in a way that will avoid recurrence of the same problems or new ones over the long term. It is when you find yourself solving the causes of problems most of the time that your organization makes real progress.

What actions were taken to effectively implement the solution? If it results in major change there should have been a pilot phase and formal review of impact on performance. Finally, learn from the situation by recording the result of implementing this solution and the implications for using this solution again in the future.

Section 12

SALES MANAGEMENT, AND GETTING THE MOST OUT OF SALESPEOPLE

Introduction

The topic of sales came up early in this book, and it seems appropriate to go back to the management side of sales to finish up. In the end we get asked more questions about how you make sales than any other. After all, whatever we think of the sales force, they are the people who initiate a lot of the business deals that organizations transact. Indeed, almost every meeting that you go to is likely to have a sales or marketing angle because if it does not you should question if the meeting is necessary in the first place.

Question 86 *What changes have happened in the sales and marketing management function over the last few years?*

The general competitive pressures in business continue to ratchet up. Productivity increases, technological innovation and the emergence of new players in the business of producing commodities, all combine to increase the pressure on marketing people to find new areas for growth and salespeople to take on higher and higher targets.

Then there is globalization. The move towards global brands and international account management has been steady over the long term but is getting faster and faster.

So the marketing function has to research much more widely and build communications and feedback systems from remote countries. The need for co-ordination emphasizes also the need for a marketing strategy that is understood and accepted by all parts of the business.

Salespeople in their turn need to build international account plans and it is their job as much to sell these internally as it is to sell them to the customer.

The main problem that concerns both functions is that of differentiation. Commodity sales, such as the hardware that makes up computers and workstations, have lower and lower margins as the basic product becomes a commodity.

The performance angle

The gross margin for hardware in the computer industry has dropped from 55% to somewhere between 15% and 20% over the last 20 years. This change has brought havoc to the sales and marketing function. They are either going to be a commodity broker buying and selling components or complete systems to a market whose sole differentiator is price, or they are going to discover new ways of adding value to the basic product.

Added value one day can be a simple industry standard the following day; so the other big change to the sales and marketing function is the need for huge flexibility, the welcoming of retraining and learning new skills and the ability to accept that doing your job well tomorrow will not be the same as doing it well today.

Question 87   *How should the role of sales be perceived in organizations?*

Many organizations fear their salespeople. They seem to be young for the money they can make and often only come to the attention of the rest of the company if something has gone wrong and, for example, a company is spending time and money trying to deliver a salesperson's promises. Nowadays, it is vital to remove this fear and replace it with a wary respect for the salespeople doing the front line job. There is a cultural point here with the USA having gone further down the line in this regard than Europe.

Build respect by, in the first place, dividing the selling job into 'hunting' or 'farming'. Hunting is about bringing in new customers, farming about increasing the amount and type of business you do with your existing customers. The skills are different and a major factor in people selection is to consider how much of each activity the job involves.

For hunters the main requirement is for persistence and the ability to take knocks. Theirs is the job that has them trying to get interviews with strangers who may not only be unaware of their need but also be antagonistic to an unsolicited approach whether on the telephone or personally.

Hunters generally work quickly, have short attention spans and feel very dissatisfied if complications of product or decision-making processes intrude on their getting to the point of closing a sale. They are opportunists and in most cases need watching to make sure that the product being sold is suitable and will work to the promises made by the salesperson.

Some would say that it is the hunters who give salespeople a bad name. There is some truth in that, but they are also the people who make innovation possible and *en masse* bear a lot of responsibility for driving the dollar round in a growth economy.

The hunter is the salesperson who gets a high level of job satisfaction in getting a first order from a new customer. A seller of reprographics expressed it like this: 'You actually have to start by getting yourself invited into the buyer's office. Then you must convince a probable sceptic that what you are offering has benefits over continuing with the people he or she has previously done business with.

'Then you have to find a project, bid for it and win it. The great feeling is that you made it happen. Unless you had made the first move and then followed through, that company would have remained loyal to its existing suppliers.'

This is the typical conversation of a hunter. You will recognize some other phrases and sayings in their coffee break chat – 'I thought I'd do one more door', 'stitched him up in no time flat.'

Many people find the prospect of doing the hunting job as horrendous, and organizations are recognising more and more their dependence on such people.

Every salesperson has to have some of the hunter attributes. A good farmer who hates or claims to be bad at new business selling may be too slow to go for the order or not sufficiently assertive to win against the competition. Once again we see the balance that is crucial for a professional account manager, between hustling to get things done and farming for the long-term.

Farmers develop skills in long-term relationship building and deep knowledge of a customer's business. A professional sales team selling machine tools, for example, will build over the years a database of customer knowledge that the customer himself may envy. The benefits to management of professional farmers come in terms of predictable orders, competitive intelligence, market changes and much more.

In FMCG (fast-moving consumer goods) this knowledge is equally important. The account manager needs to know the detail of the customer's strategy and interface to the consumer.

He or she then needs to know the results of market research and of course of actual sales. The more he or she knows about how the customers sell the product, the more able he or she is to make innovative proposals and achieve stretching sales targets.

The process angle

An aiming point of professional account management is to be able to hold a joint planning session. The sales team works with the customer to build a plan for the next year in detail, and three years in outline.

When this happens it is a sure sign that your company has truly created the 'working partnership' and 'added value'. A lot of salespeople talk about these con-

cepts but misunderstand the difficulties and timescales involved in setting the part-nership up and adding real value.

Organizations that recognize the value of such customer relationships will rightly put a lot of influence into the hands of the salespeople responsible for it and value them highly. They are, after all, considerably affecting the whole strategy of the business.

Question 88   What is the impact of technology on marketing?

This is a huge question. Many facets of it are answered in a variety of questions in this book. Perhaps the best answer is to say that you should look for technological progress in every part of the marketing function. Here is an example of some of the activities within the marketing function, along with the skills and knowledge needed to carry them out.

Table 12.1   Skills and techniques needed in the marketing function.

Marketing topic	Examples of skills and techniques needed	Examples of knowledge needed
Create a customer-focused analysis of our capabilities and opportunities	SWOT analysis Customer attribute analysis Team planning	Economic trends Technology trends Regulatory trends Competitive environment Customer environment
Defining the company purpose and the marketing strategy	Lateral thinking Long-term planning	What is happening in our chosen markets? What capabilities do we need to be successful?
Market segmentation	Techniques for segmenting markets Documentation methodologies	What type of selling does each segment need? What is the current focus and profitability of each sector?
Goal setting	Producing relevant performance measures Goal setting and documentation Making a business case	What resources are available? What external organizations can help? Calculating return on investment
Action planning	Documenting and maintaining plans Allocating accountability	

The challenge is to assess the impact of technology in every single one of those areas from using the Internet to gain information on trends to using the intranet to document plans and make them available to the entire organization.

Question 89   *What are the key principles of creating a successful sales and marketing strategy?*

- Organizations and teams should have a clear and appropriate strategic framework, along with efficient and effective operations. One without the other will lead to long- or short-term failure.
- There should be a balance between short- and long-term activity and resource allocation.
- The degree of detail, and the extent to which the framework is prescriptive as opposed to opportunistic, should be controlled by the management team and influenced by the degree of uncertainty in the external and competitive environments.
- The strategic choices considered when formulating marketing strategy will be bound by the external and competitive trends over which there is no control, and any constraints placed on the team by 'owners'.
- There is no predefined timeframe over which the marketing team should consider planning (annual planning is typically the result of accounting convenience). Instead, it should be defined by the degree and rate of change in the environment in which the team competes.
- All stakeholders should be identified and their degree of influence and extent of impact on the marketing strategy considered.
- All organizations need to have at least one unique source of differentiation from competition – this must be identified, built up and protected at all costs.
- There will be a number of choices faced by the team over the duration of the framework, and whilst all options cannot and should not be defined when formulating the strategy, the criteria by which choices will be made, and the development priorities, should be decided.
- Where a diverse set of products and services are offered, or a diverse set of markets and customers are served, it should be clear where the synergy between them is, as this will help to maximize revenues whilst maintaining costs.
- Not all product segments, and not all market segments, will be equally important. Product and market boundaries and priorities should be defined and communicated.
- Once the product and market outputs or deliverables have been defined, the organization should be designed to ensure optimum efficiency and effectiveness in terms of actually achieving the plan. The framework should therefore include the key implementation activities to make it happen!
- Before committing to changes to the strategy, risks should be considered and the potential adverse impact assessed.
- Whilst a lot of thought and analysis is put into creating marketing plans it is still necessary to monitor key indicators that will identify whether

the strategy is correct and whether it is being implemented. It should not result in a report that sits on the shelf or is put away in a drawer.

- The strategy should provide the framework by which operational decisions are made, and by which the organization is managed. The strategic framework, and the key strategic indicators, should be reviewed formally by the senior team (where the focus is not on short-term operational or functional issues).

Question 90   *Do salespeople actively tailor their marketing strategies to local requirements, when they are selling across borders?*

This is a problem that can only be addressed with the help of people in different countries. For example, there is a huge difference in the way French business people operate and the French consumer market works, and the way things happen in Spain, despite their physical closeness and the fact that they have been doing business with each other for hundreds of years. Now transpose this to the 'global village' and you get a good idea of the problem.

Look for bridges into new markets, other enterprises with whom you can create joint ventures or new marketing channels but never underestimate the cross-border differences in your market.

The people angle

This cross-border and cultural angle is a good opportunity for the human resources department to add value. Through their contacts with their opposite numbers in different countries, they can draw a profile of what is and what is not done in selling and in hiring salespeople.

Question 91   *How do companies deal with channel conflict that arises due to use of multiple channels?*

Sometimes this problem is more in the minds of the legal department than it is in the minds of those running the channels and those supplying the products. Yes, arbitrage can be deadly when one channel is for example undercutting another in sales of the same products. Therein lies the clue. Identify clearly what is the added value of each individual channel and then explain that to other channels so that they can see the differentiators that they and the other channels have.

The performance angle

A company is selling a software platform that allows organizations to tailor it to solve their particular problems and maximize their opportunities. For example, one may employ the tool as a method of controlling change projects, whilst another channel can deploy the tool in the training of salespeople and sales managers. You can clearly see the added value that these two channels bring to the tools, and as long as enough thought is given in the choice and creation of new channels the company should avoid conflict.

On the other hand, many managers are disappointed in the inability of the multiple channels that their products are sold through to cross-sell and help each other with the development of their businesses. This is because the channels focus on their own market segments and this leads them away from the activities of their colleague channels.

Question 92   In case of multiple channels, who should take the ownership of key accounts and how should these accounts be serviced?

Normal account management techniques would say that there should be an account manager for each large customer who may be served through many channels. Plainly the channel manager is responsible for the day-to-day running of their customers, but this should be in the context of an account plan supervized by the account manager.

The account manager needs to prepare this plan, and review and update it on a regular basis. It is the planning mechanism that ensures a consistent strategy is presented to the customer across all the channels. The key is to get the right resources at the planning meeting. This will include representatives from marketing as well as the channel managers. This ensures that the strategy is not only consistent for the customer across channels but is also consistent with the organization's overall plan. It is very useful also to have a senior manager as an account sponsor. Their presence at part, if not all, of the planning meeting gives the account manager the leverage he needs to get the resources to implement the plan.

Don't forget the attendance of the customer at this meeting as well. You may bring them in for a presentation of the plan, or even have them there throughout the planning event if both sides get value out of that.

The process angle

If a full blown planning session seems out of the question with your customer, consider the next best thing. Get the account team to do an analysis of the strengths, weaknesses, opportunities and threats that it thinks the customer is facing. Then take the result to the customer for verification. Almost any manager will look at such a document and, perhaps despite themselves, help to improve the accuracy and depth of information. Most people will find such an exercise interesting, and if they have not done that type of analysis themselves may be very enthusiastic. That way the team has the customer's perception of the situation to start their planning process.

Question 93   What is the right compensation strategy for salespeople to avoid discounting?

If the sales force is on a straight commission on sales then they are less than 100% motivated to get orders at list price. If you do not reflect the drop in profits caused by discounting in their compensation package, a 10% discount on the sales price has little impact on the salesperson's income but may reduce bottom line profit by more than 33%. If it is easy to administer, a lot of sales managers use the gross profit of a deal as the basis for sales bonuses, and this works quite well. The other possibility is to discount the sales bonus pro rata to the sales discount, so 90% of list price will yield, say, only 50% of the full sales bonus.

Section 13

SOME THOUGHTS ABOUT THE REAL WORLD OF BUSINESS

Introduction

There is a notice on the door of an IT division of a large business that states: 'There is strictly no admittance into this section of the building for anyone except members of the IT department.' One could be forgiven for questioning the ability of the people who penetrate this inner sanctum to provide an IT service that is directly linked in to the strategy, opportunities and problems of the corporation they are meant to serve.

Technology has been instrumental in making massive improvements in organizational productivity and customer service; but it also causes huge amounts of frustration to both employees and customers. There are, for example, many, many ways of finding incompatibilities between hardware and software that cause problems; and that number does not seem to decrease with time.

It is also true in other parts of the business that common sense seems to lose out in the practical world to corporate chaos. This is the real world putting barriers between managers and their potential to be successful. Here are some questions on that theme.

Question 94   *Why are IT projects always late and over budget?*

IT projects are often poorly planned in the first place with insufficient levels of detail and poor understanding of the business. This is compounded by the fact that the project sponsor is unaware of technical issues and driven by short-term business pressures. Put simply – 'we want it now!'

Once the project is underway, there is also little (or overly optimistic) feasibility and risk management, and the project is typically overly reliant on specialists with 1001 other tasks on the go.

To be fair to IT people a software project is very difficult to estimate simply because, by definition, they are doing something that has not been done before. It seems to work best where there is a very good liaison person driving the project. They need to have experience of the actual business in order to make their best contribution, and for that reason are often seconded out of the field on a project basis or for a length of time to do the job of IT/business interface.

The people angle

The concept of internal account managers for each department in the business can help with this. Take a business expert, a banker if you are a bank, and give them just sufficient IT knowledge to be able to converse with IT people at the business/IT communication level. Then make them responsible for IT projects.

Question 95   *How do you protect your intellectual property rights?*

This one should, strictly speaking, be answered by a lawyer; but here are some items of explanation and definition.

All written work is automatically copyrighted to the author under international law. However, it is advisable to get into the habit of placing the copyright symbol on all material that is of a sensitive nature or that will be used outside your organization. Formal contracts with customers, suppliers and employees are sometimes also advisable when dealing with commercially sensitive and valuable information.

You can also protect intellectual property by simply making it more difficult for people to take or to copy. Think about who has access to it, where it is stored and whether it is password protected. Don't try and protect everything, but get into the habit of recognising what type of information is more valuable to the business or its competitors, and place greater emphasis on protecting it. Finally, take time to make sure that people at all levels of the business understand the importance of intellectual property, what it is, and how they can add to and protect it.

Question 96   *What are business fads and should we follow them?*

This is part of a big question of fashion and herd-like movement. Everyone agrees that the stock market moves on totally emotional grounds like a herd of sheep. Some people, known as contrarians, agree that there is money to be made out of going against any popular fad in buying and selling shares. There may well be a parallel in running a business. Take two strategic fads, the one to diversify in the '80s, and go back to core business in the '90s.

If you had been a contrarian in the '80s you would have gone into the '90s with a fit slimmed-down business with its eye on its own best focus. This would probably have made you recession-proof in the debacle of the early '90s, with enough debt but not too much and so on. If, however, you had gone against the tide in the '90s, you would have had strong growth in that time but missed out on the revolution that increased the spend on IT and gave huge productivity and customer service benefits.

Unfortunately the best answer to this question is:

- keep abreast of business fads
- study those you feel might benefit your operation
- follow the ones that make objective business sense and leave the rest to the dedicated followers of fashion.

Question 97　*Why don't operations and salespeople get on?*

This is a rather negative way of asking about the natural tension between the sales force and the rest of the operation who are responsible for delivering what the salespeople have sold. When this tension becomes friction the damage it can do to a company can be very dramatic.

The people angle

A technology company had to persuade a large customer base to upgrade to its new range of hardware and software. The change gave considerable benefits to the customer but was accompanied by considerable pain in making the change. Salespeople reported back the reaction of the market and persuaded senior management that the customer needed something to cushion the blow.

The research and development department came up with an interim solution that allowed the customer to achieve, say, 40% of the benefits of the new technology and avoid the transitional pain. Salespeople and customers then fundamentally colluded, sales of the interim solution blossomed but the customer base in the long term never made the transition to the new technology and many were lost to the competition.

This is a good illustration of the strengths of a sales force in giving a company good customer feedback and also the weaknesses of most salespeople, which is to adopt the line of least resistance.

So how do you make the tension work? There is a stick and carrot approach. The stick is to make sure that the processes a salesperson has to go through to get permission to make a sale are up to date and fool proof. Persuade the salesperson to hold the company line and strategy as strongly as they can and not to cave in to simple customer pressure, often part of a customer/supplier negotiation.

The carrot is to encourage excellent communication between operations and sales and demonstrate frequently that the organization does respond to salespeople's fears when it is in the customer's interests and within the organization's strategy.

Question 98   *Who do CEOs share their problems with when they do not have any peers?*

There seems to be no doubt that everyone including the chief executive needs an arbiter or an assertive mentor.

A very successful duo of businessmen worked together as joint chief executives and built a solid successful business, despite warnings from others, including venture capitalists, that every business needs someone with an edge, either by job title or by shareholding. If you looked more closely, however, you found that there was an arbiter, or at least another person involved in the decision-making process. This person played the role of non-executive, and low paid, chairman. During planning sessions the chairman would force the two people through a route of logic that would often reveal to the more impetuous of the two that the way forward he was advocating was not right for the business as a whole. Indeed this became such a feature of the behaviour of the team that he would often at the end of such a discussion turn on his partner in mock rage saying: 'There you are, I told you it wasn't a good idea' – his way of backing down.

If you are chief executive of a small or a large business you need at least a simulation of this arbiter role. It doesn't matter who it is, your accountant, your spouse, your eldest child or your bank manager; have someone in whom you confide and who can tell you in your face that you are about to drop a clanger. (On second thoughts, probably not your bank manager. They are more concerned with avoiding trouble and potential bad debts than encouraging the green shoots of commerce. If the business takes three years to really get going and prosper, they won't be there to see it happen anyway.)

The people angle

Robert Townsend, the ex-CEO of Avis, had a wife who helped with this role, as well as an ally in the senior ranks of the business. His wife famously made him think about his role as the Director of Strategic Planning in one of his companies by saying: 'And what did you plan today, dear?' His feisty sidekick on being told of a rather hairy diversification Townsend was proposing said: 'I don't know what you call that, but we Polacks call it pissing in the soup.'

Question 99   *How do you stop internal politics dictating to the business?*

Recognize, first of all, that in the case of a lot of your people, probably the majority frankly, you will never remove the intriguing and self-oriented planning of your middle and senior managers. The antidote to these politics poisoning the performance of the business is to encourage teamwork and team identification. If the whole team is successful its members are successful.

When you recognize that internal politics are causing a problem step in and act firmly.

The people angle

A logistics manager was copied by two of his people on a series of e-mails showing a disagreement in the way a particular issue should be handled – typical internal politics. Eventually he invited the two individuals to meet him in a conference room without their knowing that the other person was going to be there. He had arranged for coffee, croissants and Danish and instructed the two people that they could not leave the room until they had an agreed way forward on the issue.

It pays to be realistic about internal politics. Yes, you have to prevent its doing the organization harm but, of course, internal politics arise from ambition, a trait that you want to encourage. Besides this, for many people, it's the best part of going to work. Try to control and channel it because you will never cut it out. After all, none of the senior managers in your organization made it without a certain amount of gossiping and strategic manipulation.

Question 100   *Do I need my customer to like me?*

People have often said that they do not care if the customer, internal or external, likes them or dislikes them, as long as they respect them. Maybe so, but in the end people buy from people not from organizations, whether they have the utmost respect for them or not. In our view having your customer disliking you is likely to be a temporary situation – either they will change suppliers or your organization will change you. The whole selling job becomes much easier when both parties like and respect each other. That way, both sides will take the rough with the smooth.

Section 14

GLOSSARY OF FREQUENTLY USED BUSINESS TERMS

360 feedback A process of obtaining feedback from your boss, colleagues and direct reports

5 forces Model for analysing relative power within an industry – research by Michael Porter

7 habits Habits exhibited by success teams – research by Steven Covey

ABC Activity based costing – a means of apportioning all costs to individual projects, product lines or markets

ASP Application service providers – providing services over the Internet and charging as and when they are used

Assumptions Beliefs that people have that underpin a plan or decision

Balanced scorecard Performance indicators used to report on how well a project, process or team is performing

BCG matrix Graph for products showing market attractiveness and competitive position – Boston Consulting Group

Belbin Model for assessing the roles that people play most naturally within teams

Benchmarking Comparing the performance and operations of one business or team with another – sometimes the best performer

Best practice Business methods and processes that reflect the most effective and efficient way of doing things

BPR Business process re-engineering – redesigning and changing business processes

Brainstorming Group idea generation activity

Brand The interpretation customers have of the image and logo of the business

Budgets Estimates of funding requirements for a team or activity

Business drivers Trends in the industry or business environment that will impact what a company does and how it does it

Capabilities Skills and resources that enable a company to satisfactorily deliver products and services to its customers

CI Continuous improvement

COGS Cost of goods sold – how much it costs to produce products and services sold to customers

s Reaching a decision that everyone is willing to commit to

Printed and bound by CPI Group (UK) Ltd, Croydon, CR0 4YY

13/04/2025

Copyright   Protection of printed or published work – automatically applies to any original piece of work

Cost-benefit analysis   Comparison of the value of a project or idea with the cost of its implementation

Critical path   Activities in a project plan where a delay will impact the overall duration of the project

CRM   Customer relationship management – the process of maximising customer satisfaction

Culture   Attitudes and behaviours that influence the way in which activities are performed

CVA   Customer value analysis – method of understanding customer purchasing criteria

DCF   Discounted cash flow – placing a value on forecasted future profits considering time and risk factors (see NPV)

Delegation   Handing over responsibility for a task to others

Dependencies   Relationships between activities in a project plan

DREC   Four stages of individual change: denial, resistance, exploration and commitment

E-commerce   Conducting business over the Internet (same as e-business)

EDI   Electronic data interchange

Emotional intelligence   People's willingness and attitude towards applying the knowledge and skills they have

ERM   Employee relationship management – the process of maximising customer satisfaction

ERP   Enterprise resource planning – electronic information used in the management and control of a business

FBD   Fact-based decision

FMEA   Failure mode and effect analysis

Forcefield analysis   Comparison of supporting and opposing forces for a new idea or project

GAAP   Generally accepted accounting principles

Gantt chart   Graphic representation of project activities against a timeline

Gate   Events in a project plan where formal go/no-go decisions are made

HTML   Hypertext mark-up language

Incumbent   The company that currently dominates an industry

Innovation   Finding new and creative products and services, or ways of doing things

Insights   New information of value to the person or others

Insurgent   A new-fast growing organization

Internet   Network transferring electronic information across computers around the world

Intranet   Network transferring electronic information across computers within an organization

IP   Internet protocol – the standards used for the transfer of information across the internet or intranet

IPR   Intellectual property rights – protection of an idea or design associated with original work

KPIs   Key performance indicators

Leadership   Providing direction and helping others achieve objectives

Leverage   Opportunities to get additional value from a capability by combining it or using it in a different way

Logistics   Resources and capabilities necessary to deliver a product or service

Marcomms   Marketing communications

Market capitalization   The total value of an organization – calculated by multiplying the total number of issued shares by the current share price

Marketing   The process of positioning a product in its target market

Milestone   Events in a project plan where progress and performance is formally monitored

Moments of truth   Those interactions, of the many interactions between a company and its customers, which really impact on the customer's perception of the company.

Myers Briggs   Method of assessing people's natural behaviours using four dimensions

Nemawashi   The process of gaining consensus to a new idea or plan

Network diagram   Graphic representation of project activities and their interrelationship

NLP   Neuro-linguistic programming – a way of changing the way people think and behave

NPD   New product development

NPV   Net present value – a calculation of profitability assessed against perceived risk levels

Patents   Formal protection of a unique idea or design for a product or method

PERT   Program evaluation review technique – network diagram showing best and worst case estimates

Portfolio   A collection of products or projects that can be assessed as a group

Problem solving   Technique used to find the root cause of something that is not working or not working as expected

Product market matrix   Two dimensional matrix plotting product and market segments, and showing relative emphasis

Quality   Meeting customer expectations (fit-for-purpose) or number of defects/rejects

Report   Method of presenting information in a format that enables analysis by others

Risks   Potential problems associated with a decision or course of action

RoI Return on investment – a calculation of how much benefit is achieved from investing money in something

S curve Graph used in marketing to denote the pattern of market take-up of a new product

SAFE Selection criteria: suitable, acceptable, feasible and enduring

Scenario planning A method of forecasting alternative future situations and assessing the likely impact on the business or team

Segmentation A way of placing products, services or markets into natural groups

SMART Objectives that are: specific, measurable, achievable, relevant and timed

Stakeholders People that are involved in or impacted by a change or decision

Strategy Framework that defines a business's or team's products, markets and the basis on which they compete

Supply chain The series of activities or businesses which in total deliver products and services to market (see Value chain)

SWAG Strategic wide angled guess, or Sophisticated wide-arsed guess – referring to decisions made with insufficient information

SWOT Analysis technique that captures: strengths, weaknesses, opportunities and threats

Synergy Gaining additional value by combining resources or opportunities

TQM Total quality management

Transformation Significant business or team change

USP Unique selling proposition – the one aspect of a product or service that makes it different to its competition

Value chain Different parts of an organization's activities that contribute to the creation of products and services (see Supply chain)

Values Beliefs and principles that guide how a person or team behaves

Work breakdown Project activities laid out in a logical grouping

KEN LANGDON has worked for many major computer companies worldwide, including Hewlett Packard and DEC, and is presently the non-executive chairman for SofTools, a supplier of electronic Integrated Support Systems, and Glenhurst Ltd, an air conditioning supplier and contractor. His books include *Key Accounts are Different* and a contribution to the *The FT Handbook of Management*, as well as books in Capstone's *Smart* and *Express Exec* series.

ANDREW BRUCE is currently the Chief Executive of SofTools Limited. SofTools has developed a leading-edge web-based platform sold under licence through strategic partners to companies such as Nokia, Centrica and Bayer. Andrew has written *Strategic Thinking*, *Project Management*, *Customer First*, and *Do-It-Now!* for the *Dorling Kindersley Essential Manager series* and is co-author of *Creating a Market Sensitive Culture.*

The complete Capstone Reference series:

The Capstone Encyclopaedia
The Complete Small Business Guide
Business FAQs

ULTIMATES:
The Ultimate Book of Business Brands (new edition)
The Ultimate Book of Business Gurus (new edition)
The Ultimate Book of Business Thinking (new edition)
The Ultimate Strategy Library (new)
The Ultimate Book of Business Breakthroughs
The Ultimate Book of Business Creativity
The Ultimate Book of Business Quotations

INDEX

Printed and bound in the UK by
CPI Antony Rowe, Eastbourne